The Boeing Gypsies

The Families Behind the

Minuteman Missile Program

D1521727

Myrna Messer

To

My granddaughters Sofia, Juliet, and Allie and my great grandson, Matthias who make it all worthwhile.

Dedication

This book is dedicated to all those "Boeing Gypsies" whose families moved together through five different states, 40 t0 60 years ago, on the Boeing's Minuteman Missile Program. I want to thank all those who gamely searched their long-ago memories and contributed their treasured stories. Without them there would be no book.

And out came the boxes!

PROLOGUE

The Minuteman Missile Days took place during the Cold War era after the Soviet Union successfully launched into orbit the world's first satellite, Sputnik. Ham radio operators in the US listened as Sputnik's mechanical beep passed overhead. Soon Americans in their living rooms heard Sputnik's transmission via radio and TV news flashes. This was very frightening for us Americans as Russia could likely now also propel a missile toward a target thousands of miles away with little or no notice. Newspapers headlines screamed that the US must catch up with the Soviets or we would be dead. This accelerated public pressure to so something more.

In 1958, America began developing what has become the mainstay of America's defense-the Minuteman Missile. (The Titan and the Atlas ICBM came before.) That same year, the Air Force announced that Boeing would lead the program to build, test, and deploy the missile. Under the direction of the mighty US Air Force, public and private engineers dove deeply into their research to develop their solid-state missile program, an advanced-type of intercontinental ballistic missile (ICBM) called the Minuteman Missile to be land based and stored vertically in underground silos. This solid-state fuel missile could be launched from an unmanned silo in a moment's notice and would accelerate so quickly that it could fly out of its silo and through its exhaust flames and not be damaged.

 This Minuteman Program evolved into 1000 missiles in six locations in five rural American states- North Dakota, South Dakota, Montana, Wyoming and Missouri, which also covered Nebraska and Colorado sites. (This formidable force has shrunk to 400 Minuteman missiles as of 2017.) It was in these states that the Boeing Gypsies lived, worked, and played.

Williston, North Dakota 1958

I was teaching 6th Grade in Williston, ND in 1956 and had a long, lanky student who loved to shoot hoops at recess. I was playing on a city basketball team, and I used to shoot baskets with him and other kids. That young man's name was Phil Jackson, who soon played college basketball at the University of North Dakota. Phil then went on to play professionally with the New York Knicks. He coached the Chicago Bulls to six NBA titles. He retired after being Coach of the Year in 1997 and returned to in 1999 to coach the Los Angeles Lakers to three more NBA titles. (And to think I shot baskets with him!) After reading his book "Sacred Hoops", I wrote him a note of congratulations and was surprised to receive a hand-written Thank You note, which included reminiscences about being my 6th grade student.

My friend Maisie and I were out dancing at the American Legion Club, which we frequently did, when a fellow asked me to dance. He introduced himself as Archie Bartosh and said he was in town working with a Mobil Oil Seismograph crew. During the waltz, he asked me where I was from, and I told him Minot, then corrected myself by saying, "Well, actually, I'm from a town near Minot but it's so small that you wouldn't have heard of it." "What small town?" he persisted. When I told him Foxholm, a look of amazement crossed his face. "I work with fellow whose wife Val was from Foxholm." I knew everyone in and around my hometown and told him quite emphatically that he must be mistaken as there was no one by that name. When he kept insisting, it finally dawned on me that he was talking about Valetta Ahmann who married Ken Tait, an engineer with Mobil Oil. The next song, Ray, curious to know who knew Val, asked me to dance. That was the beginning of our dancing together for the next 63 years.

Sheridan, Wyoming

We were married that summer and lived as newly-weds in Williston three whole weeks before Ray was transferred to Sheridan, Wyoming, which is nestled down between the Big Horn Mountains. It was a beautiful area with no wind. No wind was a big change for us. When it snowed, our yard looked like a picture on a Christmas card. The fluffy snow would quietly pile up on the fence posts and trees making it look like a fairyland. Little Goose Creek ran beside the little furnished apartment that we rented and on the other side of that stream was a small city zoo. Every morning, Major, the lion, would wake us up. One afternoon I looked out and standing in front of Major's cage was an Indian woman who was openly nursing her baby while others milled around close by. I didn't understand the Indian culture.

Our apartment was in the back part of our landlord's house. Louie Paul was an eccentric old man who lived by himself. His bib overalls hung loosely on his body, which appeared to be slowly withering away, his glasses were always slightly askew and he always wore a jaunty brown hat that was cocked over one eye. One morning about 6 o'clock, I was awakened by a loud rapping noise on the door. (Ray was working out of town.) When I opened it, there stood a very loudly distraught Louie, "I know what you're trying to do! You're trying to take away my driver's license!" Louie was still in his house when we moved, but I would guess not for long.

Eloise lived in our backyard in an apartment over Louie's garage. She was a regal "old maid", (63 was old to us) who worked at the courthouse. (When I watched the Downton Abbey series, I told Ray, "There's Eloise!" The Dowager Countess Violet could have been her model.) She didn't own a car, never had, and walked the ten blocks to work, rain or shine. In the winter she'd bundle up in scarfs, mittens, and snow pants and when she got to work, she would change into her business attire, which she carried in a satchel over her arm. She had a birth defect, a relatively large hump on her left shoulder, which caused her to walk slightly stooped over. It didn't, however, detract from her elegant demeanor; she was always "Violet."

Eloise was partial to suits and often wore a stylish one with a silk blouse tied in a bow at her neck. When she invited us for dinner, she merely replaced her jacket for an apron but the rest remained the same. The table was set with fine China and silver and I remember she made simple, yet refined, tapioca pudding served in crystal stemmed bowls. For us, it was fine dining.

Never having had children of her own, Eloise "adopted" us. She often called us over for a "little glass of wine" and glorious stories, many of which were about "Coffee Dan" who lived in Seattle and to whom, she inferred, she was engaged. As long as we lived there, we never saw a sign of "Coffee Dan" so we wondered, "Was he was just fantasy or the real thing?"

We loved the mountains and spent many weekends in them. Ray would fish and I read and sat on the rocks that jutted out of the meandering mountain streams. Of course, we picnicked. We wanted to bottle up those special days and take them with us.

We took many drives through those beautiful mountains. I remember one drive vividly. We climbed slowly, savoring every mile of our scenic tour, and came back down fast, very fast. Our car had no power brakes, and as we descended, our speed increased and we shot down the mountain road, despite of Ray's attempt to slow down. The brakes had become heated, decreasing their braking power. It was one of our most, shall I say, exhilarating rides that we ever took.

Many of the old movie stars also loved the mountains and had cabins in them. Robert Taylor was one of them. He came into town often enough that the locals treated him as one of them. One morning Verna Kubik, whose husband Art also worked for Mobil Oil, and I saw him going into a grocery store. We quickly needed groceries, too, and fell into the checkout line behind him and waited as the clerk checked him out. He was as ruggedly handsome in person in his jeans and black cowboy hat as he was on the screen. We prided ourselves for not screaming and throwing ourselves on him.

Jerry Cookson, who also worked with Ray, and his wife Jeanette, introduced us to the game of bridge, which we've been playing for 63 years and still learning. Jeanette was as different from her husband as night and day. Jerry was quiet, well-educated and grew up in a large city. Jennette who grew up in Dickinson, North Dakota in a blue-collar family, was loud, fun-loving, rather coarse and endearing. We had much in common...until it came to house-keeping and drinking coffee. She was fanatically clean (OCD) while I was just clean, and she liked her coffee lukewarm while I drank mine hot. I remember the first time she came for coffee. She glanced down at it and then let it sit and sit before she even took a sip. I thought for sure I had botched my new role as hostess. We drank many cups together after that first time, and I found that I hadn't failed after all.

I bowled in a local bowling league and occasionally teams would volunteer to go to the Veteran's Hospital, which was located in the foot hills of the mountains near Sheridan, and bowl against the patients in the psychiatric ward. Our team took its turn and we spent a very interesting evening at the VA Hospital.

I had become acquainted with two elderly sisters who were North Dakota natives. They didn't drive anymore and wanted to go back to Bismarck to see relatives. Knowing I was from North Dakota, they asked me if I would be interested in driving them. Since Ray had his vacation coming up, I decided to go and Ray would follow two weeks later. Sheridan was celebrating All American Indian Days and there was a lot of action downtown. Ray, being a Bachelor-For-A-Day, went down to the Legion Club for dinner, where we often went to dance to the music of Bud Benth. He and a friend Rex Leet, stopped on their way home to watch some of the activities from the grandstand. He remembers a guy on a loudspeaker reminding people to stick around for the big dance that was to follow. (The big dance turned out to be an Indian Tribal Dance, a very different kind of dance than what those two greenhorns thought it would be.) When Ray pulled out of the parking lot on his way home, a drunken reveler smashed into him and totaled our car. He came to pick me up in a new Buick Super Hardtop. Ray left for "the field" on Monday morning and returned on Thursday night. (He sometimes worked as far as 200 miles away.) I had left my teaching job, and with time on my hands, I decided to go back to college. When I went to enroll in the junior college, I found that the only class I could get that I didn't have was History of Wyoming. So, I applied to substitute (There is just so much coffee drinking one can do.) and was soon sent out to rural schools.

Creating seismograph shock wave

One assignment was in a one-room school 40 miles southeast of Sheridan at Ucross, which got its name from a prominent cattle company in that area whose brand was a U with a cross beneath it. (The students enjoyed telling me the story.) It was to be a week-long assignment. The teacher I was subbing for stayed in the teacherage during the week, so I did too.

When I arrived for my week's adventure, I took one look and immediately set about making some sense out of chaos that greeted me. When I found out there was to be a Grange meeting in the school that week, my first thought was, "Something has to be done." I dusted and cleaned and waded through the clutter of old papers and put up bulletin boards which proudly displayed the work we did, including fun art projects. The students who ranged in age from six to thirteen were eager to help and couldn't wait for their parents' reactions when they came for the meeting. When the night came, not realizing that I was expected to attend the meeting, I did some last-minute changes, put on the coffee and nicely retired to the teacher's quarters. Immediately, there was a knock on the door, "We're ready to start." It was my first and last Grange meeting.

And the end of the week, I started my long lonely trip home. It was a desolate road. I had driven several miles without seeing a single car or truck when suddenly, without any warning, my car died. There I was, in the middle of nowhere with a car that wouldn't run and no help in sight. I was panic-stricken! Then, lo and behold, along came a pickup. The young man (obviously a rancher) stopped, opened my hood and fiddled around with something. I turned the key and the motor roared to life. Thanking the man, I took off down the highway and never stopped until I pulled into our garage. I turned off the motor and that was it. Dead! It turned out that it never should have started there on that deserted road. A ground wire on the distributor was broken inside the insulation which he couldn't possibly have fixed. To this day, I believe it was my guardian angel who had stopped to help me.

(The Ucross teacher had to pay me herself as it was a personal leave and when I got my check, she had given me a $5.00 tip!)

I subbed in another small one-room school near Monarch which was only 15 minutes from Sheridan. Monarch was nestled in the Big Horn Mountains along the Piney Creek, and the scenery was breathtaking. Each time I made the trip, I marveled at its beauty.

The little town was founded in the early 1900's by one of the many coal companies that once operated in the area. It was ranching country, and being so far from larger towns with schools, the parents fought to keep their little school.

Once again, I had all grades, first through eighth. Since I subbed there many times, I also got to know the parents. They took turns bringing lunch for the students, which I warmed up and served at noon, and they always stayed a minute to chat.

I taught all subjects, including penmanship (Palmer Method), art, and music. I remember one little first grade boy went home and told his mother, "Boy, can that teacher ever sing." I smiled at that one.

My subbing at that little school ended up with them offering me a contract for the following year. I graciously declined as Mobil Oil was transferring us to Plentywood, Montana and, furthermore, I had just learned that I was pregnant with our first son.

Plentywood, Montana

Six weeks before our baby was born, we packed up our few belongings and headed out for Plentywood, Montana. It was the dead of winter when the sun went down at three in the afternoon and the temperatures sank to minus 20 degrees. We had found an apartment right across from the hospital and when my time came, the nervous father and I put on our snow boots and walked across the street. During that long evening of labor, the doctor told Ray that he might as well go home and catch a nap as I wouldn't deliver for hours. Seemed the baby had plans of his own and when he was born a short while later, Ray was home fast asleep. When the phone rang with the news, the new father asked, "Is the baby okay? The mother?" Assured that we were both fine, he then said, "Okay, I'll be right over."

Muskogee, Oklahoma

When Mike was only six weeks old, Mobil took us to Muskogee, OK where we traded frigid temps for tornadoes, collard greens and chiggers which were alien to all we knew.

We were happy to find a cute little house that used to be a large garage. It was remodeled using every square inch of space to transform it into an efficient modern house. The tiny kitchen had everything that one three-times its size would have. To make more counter space, the stove, when not in use, folded into the wall next to the built-in oven. This was a high-end option at that time. The windows in the living and dining room were thermo panes that were fashioned to fit into the peak of the roof creating an abundance of light and more wall space for the placement of furniture. The living room had a built-in book case with several shelves which, being avid readers, was a big plus for us and it was high enough that a chair could be placed comfortably beneath it. It was like a doll house, really. (Several years after we moved to Derby, we took a day trip to Muskogee and looked for our little house. There were several changes, even a railroad track that had been near us was all overgrown with weeds. We did find it, but it had been sorely neglected and was nearly unrecognizable. I had a lump in my throat as we turned and drove away.)

Oklahoma, at that time, was a dry state and no liquor could legally be sold. This made the distilling of liquor a thriving illegal business. Much of this was done in the back hills where the stills could be hidden easily. The Back Hills Region around Muskogee was also sought out by Mobil as it had geographical potential for oil. Before working in that location, they were warned in advance to watch out for snakes, chiggers (Ray was initiated in the chiggers, big time.) and moonshiners. The moonshiners, for obvious reasons, kept their location and activities secret. It was an absolute must that Mobil make it known right off that they were not the Feds. Once this was established, their quest for oil could go on without any problems.

According to Russell Sorrels, our land lord, the reason Oklahoma was dry was because of the bootleggers and the Baptist ministers. Russell's wife was a very strong Baptist and there was no drinking or smoking allowed in their home. Therefore, Russell, who liked a beer and a smoke, would bring his lawnmower over on Sunday morning (timed so that we would be home from Mass) and while Ray mowed the lawn, he sat and drank cold beer and smoked Camels. (There was a well-dressed black couple who used to arrive at our church in a chauffeured car. We remember because it was the only time in all our travels that we ever saw anyone being brought to Mass by a hired chauffeur.)

One of Ray's buddies dropped by one Saturday morning and asked Ray if he wanted to go down to the Rexall Drug for a cup of coffee. Upon their arrival, the waitress at the lunch counter greeted Willie with, "The usual?" At Willie's nod, she looked at Ray. "I'll have the same," my unsuspecting husband replied. It was the first time Ray had ever had a double shot of whiskey before breakfast.

Across the street from that infamous drug store was a Safeway store. Up near the front window was a display shelf that held many one-pound boxes of various brands of snuff. Being his curious self, Ray asked the manager, who happened to be standing nearby, "Who in the world buys pound boxes of snuff?" And his answer, "Little old ladies. They get together and rub it on their gums." (Being new to the South, I tucked that memory away along with the time I looked out and saw a little old Black nanny in our yard gathering dandelion greens. She was putting them into her apron, which fit in with the picture I had of the South.)

One Saturday morning, Ray took the baby and I for a ride out in the back hills and I discovered a totally different world. The drive was beautiful. There were luscious green trees, foliage and wild flowers as far as we could see. Sitting in one particularly beautiful spot was a small run-down house, surely abandoned. The door hung open on one hinge, a ragged curtain hung across a broken window, the siding was void of paint, and rusted car parts and old tires littered the yard. And then to our surprise, a young very pregnant woman carrying a small child stepped through the sagging door. At that moment, an old truck turned, in a cloud of dust, and made its way up the rutted dirt driveway. Tied to the bumper was a tire that bounced along behind. Riding in it were two little children who were obviously having the time of their lives. This was typical of what Ray and the crew saw every day while working in the back hills of Oklahoma.

Ray's company was known for its great parties. When there was an occasion to celebrate, they would scout out a place that would provide good food, music and, of course, liquor. When it became time for a party in Muskogee, finding that place became a bit of a problem as there were no clubs. After looking and looking, they finally found something that would have to do...a bare room with pale blue walls and whose ambience was created by bare light bulbs that dotted the ceiling. There were no accommodations for food or liquor so consequently, the crew dug around and found someone who would cater the food. And the liquor? Maybe they visited that waitress in the drug store. There was no dancing which had always been a must. But, when in Rome, do as the Romans do.

21

Just as we had nicely settled into life in sunny Oklahoma, Ray came home with the news that another move was in the making. This time it would be to Marfa, Texas and with a tempting promotion. We had a decision to make. Now that we had a son, the extra money would come in handy but did we want to continue moving as we had?

That evening we learned what it meant to live in "Tornado Alley". As we were finishing dinner, we heard the chilling sound of a tornado siren. An eerie green glow lit up the sky and the wind! It howled and twisted and turned as it roared through the area. Black funnel shaped clouds hovered above and then came a frightening silence. Grabbing baby Mike, we headed for our tiny bathroom where we huddled, nearly paralyzed with fear, for what seemed like hours before the all-clear signal was given.

The next day we realized just how lucky we had been. Seventeen tornadoes had touched down, all in our area. Our decision was made. We were going back to North Dakota where, when it stormed, we shut the door and turned up the heat. And, there was an added bonus- no more moving! Little did we know that our moving days were just beginning.

Minot, North Dakota

Now that we were back in our home territory and no longer moving, Ray went job hunting. A friend of his steered him towards a Casualty and Life insurance company and he became an insurance man. That didn't last long (two days, to be exact) as he didn't agree with their ethics.

Now that he was an "experienced" insurance salesman, he had no problem finding a job with a different life insurance company. Being paid strictly on commissions and even though I did some substituting in Minot, we were cinching our belts tighter and tighter. It was time for him to hang up his insurance license and find something else. This prompted another move, we packed up and moved back to Foxholm.

Ray got his first job with Boeing in 1964. He was hired by Ben Basaraba as a technician on the missile sites near Minot. When that was completed, Ben put in a good word for Ray on another job. He was hired to negotiate with landowners on how much they were to be paid by Boeing for the posts identifying the location of the communication cables that were placed underground on their land. After reaching the negotiated price, Ray then wrote the check. Carol Peterson, Ray's co-worker, was negotiating with a farmer when a neighbor who had been listening, broke in and said belligerently, "I have some of those posts on my land and I don't want them there and what's more, I'm going to tear them out!" Carol told him to do what he wanted but to remember they're government property and that it would be a federal offense. On his way to those contentious posts, the neighbor saw an Air Force Helicopter fly over. By the time Carol got to the next farmer, the contrite neighbor was already there. "I was only kidding about those posts. I'm ready to deal."

One afternoon, Ray was working on a deal with a farmer out in the middle of a wheat field near Garrison when he received a call from the head of HR. "Come in. Your son is in the Trinity Hospital with two broken arms." Five-year-old Mike had been playing in the school yard, which was adjacent to our yard, with his little cousin. They were on top of the tall slide when Mary Lynn playfully gave him a shove, causing him to topple over the side. (I can still see him coming into the house with both arms dangling.) Mary Ann, Mary Lynn's mother, took us into Minot and dropped us off at the Emergency Room. I had had to call Boeing at the base (no cell phones) to get a message to Ray to pick us up. . . The slide sat in lonely solitude for the rest of the summer.

Ben and Lois Basaraba were both from North Dakota. Lois was from Burlington which is just ten miles from Foxholm and Ben was from Belfield. My mom and dad were friends of Lois' parents, the Brockels, when they were young couples so Lois and I had that in common. Gayle, one of Ben and Lois's daughters who was a nurse, had a very interesting job. She was the nanny for the King of Jordon's youngest son and lived in the castle with them. Lois shared stories that Gayle related to them about the King, who was very relaxed at home with his family. She told about pillow fights, short-sheeting beds and other pranks that he played. A king having pillow fights and playing pranks? We were awed by it all and couldn't wait to hear about her next adventure as the Royal Prince's nanny.

When the job that Ben had gotten him was completed, Ray switched back to working on the missile sites out from the Minot Air Force Base.

Ben and Lois Basaraba and Dick Milner

In the spring of that year, there as an unusual incident that was observed in Mike Flight. Something (maybe a UFO?) was sighted hovering over Mike Six. There was a Security Camper on site with two airmen inside who called in stating that there was a very bright object hovering above the site. The Strike Team was dispatched to the site and the airmen left quickly saying, "We're out of here!" The story was related to the Boeing crew who were working on the Door Mode at the Launch Control Facility. Nothing more was said of it.

At that same time, the Malstrom AFB reported this incident: During the early morning hours of March 16, 1967, missile maintenance crews and security teams were camped out at two of the Launch Facilities and the report came in from the Security patrols and maintenance crews that they had seen UFOs that were reported to be directly above one of the silos. (It turned out that at least one security policeman was so affected by this encounter that he never again returned to missile security duty.)

The capsule alarm horn sounded at about 8:30 a.m. One of the Minuteman Missiles they supervised had gone off alert (became inoperable). The Capsule Commander was upset thinking that the maintenance personal had failed to notify him as required and that they had opened the LF (missile facility personal access hatch) that immediately breaks security. The commander quickly called the missile site and spoke with an on-site guard who reported that they hadn't yet performed any maintenance and thus had not broken security. The guard went on to tell him that they had seen a UFO hovering over the site. As the disbelieving commander was wondering what the guard was drinking, other missiles started to go off alert in rapid succession. Within minutes, the entire flight of ten ICBMs were reporting a "No-Go" condition. One by one across the board, each missile had become inoperable.

When the check list had been completed for each missile site, they found that each of the missiles had gone off-alert status due to a Guidance and Control System alert fault. Power had not been lost to the sites, the missiles simply were not operational. For some unexplainable reason, each of their guidance and control had malfunctioned. Security teams were dispatched to those sites and personal at each site reported having seen UFOs hovering over the site. It took maintenance the entire day and late into the night to bring then all back into operational status. The missiles had been lost in our deterrent forces and remained out of service for an entire day!

An equally dramatic story happened in another LCC that same morning. It was a typical clear cold Montana night sky. There were no city lights to detract from the

25

spectacular array of stars, and it was not uncommon to see shooting stars. Montana is called "Big Sky Country" for obvious reasons, and airmen on duty topside would often go outside to look for them. It was one of those airmen who first saw what appeared to be a star zigging across the sky. And then he saw another one doing the same thing, and this time it was bigger and closer. He called to his Flight Security Controller to come take a look. They both stood there watching lights streak directly above them, stop, change directions at high speed and then return overhead. They ran into the building and called The Deputy Capsule Commander, not taking the report seriously, directed him to call back if anything significant happened. A few minutes later, the security NCO called again. This time clearly frightened and was shouting that there was a red saucer-shaped UFO hovering silently outside the front gate!

While trying to make sense of what was happening, they heard the klazon alarm reverberate through the confined space of the capsule and then saw a No-Go (inoperable) light and two red security lights were lit indicating problems at one of the missile sites. Before he could check the system to determine the cause of the problem, another alarm went off at another site, and then another and another all simultaneously. Within the next few seconds, they had lost six to eight missiles to No-GO condition. Once again, the cause was not found.

It was during this time that a two-person SAT team assigned to Echo Flight was performing a routine check of the missile launch facilities a few miles north of Lewistown, Montana. As they approached one of the launch facilities, an astonishing sight caused the driver to slam on his brakes. Stunned in amazement, they watched as, about 300 feet ahead, a very large glowing object hovered silently directly over the launch facility. One of them called in and told the Commander who was on duty. The Commander didn't believe him at first but the young airman's emotional state was so obvious that he finally called the Command Post and reported it. The officer on duty at the Command Post refused to accept the report saying that they no longer recorded those kinds of reports. In other words, he didn't want to hear about the UFO. Unsure of what to tell his shaken security guard, the captain decided to give the guard permission to fire his weapon at the object if it seemed hostile. The airman told him, "Thanks sir, but I really don't think it would do any good." A few seconds later, the object flew silently away.

Declassified Strategic Missile Wing documents and interviews with ex-Boeing engineers who conducted test following the incidents confirmed that no positive cause for the missile shut-down was ever found.

We were living in Lewistown at that time. Our son Jim and some of his friends saw these same "UFOs" which were above and a little north of Lewistown. After reading the accounts about them, Jim found it interesting that what he saw was very similar to what the airmen saw-three to five star-like objects that were sometimes in formation but otherwise zigzagging around. He doesn't remember them getting close, but remembers they were uniquely star-like and fairly high up, like a plane or a slow satellite. It made a lasting impression on him as it did on all who witnessed this amazing phenomenon.

Grand Forks Air Force Base

Once again, we packed up (by this time we had three little boys) and moved to the Grand Forks, ND where we lived on the air base in a trailer court set up by Boeing. There were two makes of trailers, the Magnolia and the Frontier and we were given a Magnolia. It became my preference and I felt fortunate to get one every time we lived in a Boeing trailer park.

It was a total change for all of us but, in many ways, a good change. We paid $55 a month with everything furnished, including laundry facilities and utilities. I met my good friend Sue Bitel in the wash house. (Little did we know that we would both settle down in Derby, KS) I next saw that friendly gal in the Base View Beauty Shop which was located just off the base in a little strip mall where my cousin Bill Miller managed one of the Millers' Grocery stores in Grand Forks. She told me that it was her birthday and she and her husband Ray were going out for dinner with Louie and Andy Belisle as it was also Louie's birthday. I remember feeling envious as it sounded like such fun. Again, little did I know that over the years, I would celebrate many birthdays with her, and also with Louie as he and Andy also became our special friends. Sometimes when we got together, Louie would play his concertina which always livened up the party, especially when he played a good 'ole Minnesotan polka. You betcha!

Living on the Grand Forks Air Base was a memorable experience. The day after we moved in, I enrolled Mike, a second grader, in his new school. I remember having a lump in my throat when I left him. It had been hard to take him away from his school and friends and even harder to leave him in a strange one. I put on a smile and promised to be there to pick him up when school was over. That afternoon as I drove into the school parking lot, I was surprised to see it so empty. I had gotten the dismissal time wrong and most of the students were gone, including Mike. I fought down panic and tried to think rationally. What would he do? Try to find his own way home? I hadn't seen him along the way but maybe I had missed him. I retraced my route, still no Mike. All I could think of was how frightened he must be, all alone in a strange place and no Mom. And then I saw him. He was walking through a field and was nearly home. To this day, I don't know how he made it as that field was quite a distance from the street and not easily seen, even when one was looking for it. But then, this was the same boy who became an Eagle Scout at a very young age. (You can be sure that I never made that mistake again and I enrolled my boys in many new schools during our Boeing Gypsy days.) Jack, son number two, started Kindergarten there. I was surprised that it took our little explorer three weeks before he'd go into his classroom without persuasion. (Another lump in my throat.) But his teacher assured me that as soon as I left, he was just fine, and she even gave him a compliment...he was "The Best Rester" in the whole class!

Three-year-old Jeff made the news when we lived on that base. One afternoon there was a knock on my door and there stood an Air Force security guard, "Do you have a little boy named Jeff?" While Sue and I were drinking coffee, our sons were out joy-riding on their tricycles on the flight line! That was another "never happened again."

We met a variety of couples while moving around and one of the more interesting ones was Justin and Jeanette Pendley who were our neighbors on our first Boeing move. Justin was a conservative doting husband. (I called him strange. One example-Jeanette told me that the first time he kissed her was when he proposed to her.) They had three boys who were about my boys' ages, and a darling little girl named Ramona. I became Jeanette's friend and confidant and, as I got to know her, I realized just how much she needed both.

Justin was quite religious and very intelligent. He was also the self-appointed decision maker of the family. Jeanette didn't drive and, having a big family, it made it hard for her. It was particularly difficult since she was pregnant and had to get to her doctor's appointments. That didn't seem to concern her husband as he went everywhere with her anyway and, when it came to shopping, he preferred to do it himself. (He particularly liked to shop for Ramona. Jeanette once showed me her closet which was crammed full of dozens of little dresses, all bought without her input or knowledge.)

But the most memorable of the family was little Lionel who was about four. He was a cute little guy with sharp dark eyes that sparkled with mischief and who definitely kept his mother on her toes. He liked to "fix" things with his favorite tool, his father's hammer. And fix them he did! One day he was found "helping" a maintenance man who was doing some repair work on a trailer. That was the last time Dad's hammer was ever seen. When baby Micah was born, Lionel used to climb into the crib and try to lift his little brother out so he could play with him. His mother had to watch him like a hawk and never left them alone for a minute. Jeanette was one busy harried woman who was unable to get away from her everyday stress and do the fun things that we other women took for granted. And I liked her a lot.

Dick and Toni Milner and their girls lived a couple trailers down from us and became our good friends. We spent a lot of time with the Milners and found that Toni was a very resourceful woman who could do a little of everything. For instance, it was Toni's job to take care of their TV antenna which was attached to the roof of their trailer. It was not unusual to see her

The Milners Dick, Toni, Jeni, Lisa and Amy

crawling up on their front porch to reposition it so she could watch Star Wars. She introduced Ray and I to lamb which was one of her specialties. She had grown up eating lamb as her dad had a sheep ranch in Hermosa, SD which is in the Black Hills where they live today. Toni was also a savvy card player. This was proven over and over when we played pinochle with our husbands as they went down in defeat more often than not. To this day, they claim we cheated.

In those days when we went out dancing, we went to clubs. (Moose, Legion, VFW, Elks, Eagles, and KC's) In Grand Forks, it was the Legion Club, which actually is across the Red River in East Grand Forks. Del and Betty Reimers, good friends of the Milners, often went with us. Betty, a little older than I, shared my love of cooking and we often shared recipes over a cup of coffee. And, Del? Ray remembers him from work but I remember him because he was a very good dancer! I must have worn out at least one pair of shoes dancing with him.

Toni had the knack for being in the wrong place at the right time. There was the time she and Dick were socializing in a bar in Rapid City that was managed by her dad when Indians came in swinging chains with crescent wrenches attached to them. The Indians, who were protesting what they considered too lenient treatment of a white man accused of the stabbing death of an Indian in Buffalo Gap, SD, had backed up a panel truck to the front door, jumped out and went in swinging. In her terror, Toni had jumped over the bar and broke her ankle. Four bars were heavily damaged that night and several people injured.

The thing we remember most clearly about our stay on that Grand Forks Air Base that first winter was the ice storm! It was bitterly cold and as fast as the rain came down, it froze. Everything was covered with a thick layer of ice. Branches, coated with ice and glistening like diamonds, were ripped from trees. Power lines, heavy with shimmering ice, tore loose spewing sparks as they snaked along on the ground, leaving us in total darkness. Our Mobil homes, being temporary housing, had metal siding which added an even greater risk and thus we were told to evacuate immediately. Driving to Grand Forks on glare ice was an adventure of the utmost and finding an available motel once we got there was an even greater challenge. Finally, we saw a flickering Vacancy sign. After five minutes I wondered which was worse, staying on base and suffering the consequences or freezing to death in a room where the frigid air seeped in around the windows and rolled in under the door. As we shivered and shook, Ray cranked up the wall-mounted heating unit. It gave a loud belch and that was it. And if freezing to death wasn't enough, the room reeked of cigarette smoke and the bathroom should have been condemned years before. Somehow, we survived and when we got back to the base, our trailer felt like a palace.

The Wagner's (Norm, Mary Lu, Pam, & Susan)

One storm we missed was the four-day blizzard they had in Grand Forks before we got there. Norm Wagner remembers it well. He being from Washington and Mary Lou from Texas, they must have thought that it was end of the world. It had been a nice evening, quite nice actually, when Norm set out for the grocery store. While out, he met a buddy who asked if he wanted to go bowl a couple lines. Norm, a very good bowler, was always up to bowling. After bowling a few lines, the friend asked, "Have you got time for a little poker?" Norm was also known to enjoy a little poker and so the night went. By that time, it had begun to snow and when they went out to go home, it was an all and out raging blizzard. Norm left his car with the groceries at the bowling alley and got into his friend's truck. They drove a block, got stuck and had to get out and push. They drove a little further, got stuck again and had to push, and all of this with no overshoes or heavy coats. Finally, after what seemed like forever, they reached the friend's house where Norm stopped to warm up before he set out on his final lap home...on foot. When he got to his front door, he was freezing cold and played out, and to top it all off, the groceries were still at the bowling alley. In spite of his long grueling night, Norm said he didn't get a bit of sympathy from Mary Lu.

After being completely shut down by the blizzard for four days, work resumed for the Boeing workers. Willie Diehl and a guy named Kirkland picked up a Boeing vehicle and started out to a site, all of which were miles and miles from the Dispatch Area. The roads had been plowed out, leaving banks higher than the car, restricting their vision. After driving for some time, they came to a small town that had a railroad running through it. Just as they rounded a corner and had started across the railroad crossing, they heard a loud whistle. Both of them bailed out of the car just moments before the train hit, dragging it yards down the track. For one terrifying minute, Kirkland the driver, didn't realize that Willie had jumped to safety. (If they had been wearing seatbelts as they would have today, they never would have made it.) Louie Belisle, who was on his way to that same site, was right behind them and saw it all. It was something he'll never forget.

Kirk and Dee Ann Keffler were living in East Grand Forks during that notorious snow storm and Dee Ann was nine months pregnant with their second child. She was more than a little nervous as their car was buried in snow and all the streets were blocked solid. They couldn't even get out of their house as the snow was so high that it covered their doors and windows. It took days to get the streets cleared and then there was only one lane. Friends who were more fortunate came and dug them out so if the baby decided it was time, they could at least get their car out. And then the phone rang. It was Dee Ann's obstetrician who called to tell her which hospital he was in. He told her at the first sign of labor to call the emergency number and they would send a snowmobile for her. As it turned out, they didn't need that snowmobile. Baby Twyla considerately waited till the storm abated and the roads open! And her father breathed a well-earned sigh of relief.

Ray Bitel, (husband of that friendly gal I met in the wash house) usually worked in ET&M but on occasion was sent out into the field for a couple weeks. On one of these days, Ray had a little mishap. It was the end of a long day and the work cage that was used when the men were working in the launch tube, had to be hauled up. It weighed about 200 lbs. and had to be pulled 20 ft. by hand so it was a hard job that took time. More than ready to be on his way home, Ray asked Louie Belisle, who regularly had this job, how he could speed up the removal of the cage. Louie told him to tie a rope to a car and pull. Sounded good to Ray. Just as it was near the top, it hung up on something and the rope broke. The cage landed on the bottom and was demolished! In shock, Ray thought sure he'd be fired. It just so happened that the safety chief had been after Ray to pitch on his fast pitch softball team but Ray didn't feel like playing and had turned him down.

33

The next morning after the accident, Ray went into the safety chief's office and volunteered. There was never a word said about the cage fiasco.

While our Magnolia wasn't a palace, it became home. All of the trailers were furnished with the same basic furniture and fiberglass curtains. The curtains came in two colors-gold or orange, of course to blend in with the brown-tweed upholstery. When we moved and were assigned a new trailer, we'd jokingly ask friends, "What color drapes did you get?" and sometimes in the dead of night, we'd trade. We've laughed many times remembering those fashionable drapes. Even though the trailers were basically the same, they were different in the sense that we all added our personal touches which made it ours. We celebrated many occasions in those trailers and never worried about having enough room or "just the right serving pieces" as we were all in the same boat. And today, we look back on those days and remember all the fun we had in those trailer houses...with the fiberglass orange or gold drapes that matched the brown-tweed furniture.

While living on Grand Forks Air Base, the super-secret SR71, which was the fastest plane ever built, had a mechanical problem and was forced to land on the base. Ray and a co-worker Rowdy Yates were there when several days later it lifted off, made a turn and came back across the runway at a high rate of speed. Awe struck, Rowdy commented as it went out of sight, "They're probably already calling Beale Air Force Base for landing instructions." (Beale is in Marysville, California.) The Blackbird's first test flight was on December 22, 1964 and it was never hit by a missile in the 25 years it was in service. It served an important role in history as a spy plane. It had an exceptionally low radar profile owing to its sleek needle nose and special black ferrite iron radar-absorbing paint which made the Blackbird a difficult target. Plus, its maximum speed was 2,193 m.p.h. and it could climb so high that the crew needed to wear pressure suits so as not to pass out. Also, the fuel was designed to have a safe, high-flashpoint that would not vaporize or blow up under extreme heat and pressure. The Blackbird had an impressive military record having penetrated Soviet and other communist states, plus it provided support for US bombing missions. Improved enemy air defenses capable of retaliation put an end to the Blackbird in 1990. (Coincidentally, in the late 1990's our youngest son Jim shared a commercial flight to Asia and several adult beverages with none other than Bill Weaver, the only pilot to survive a Blackbird disintegration, which happened while he was doing Mach 3.2 at 78,800 feet.)

Rapid City, South Dakota

Just before Christmas that year, Ray got the news that he and his crew were being transferred to Rapid City, South Dakota to install a Minuteman Missile training facility on the Ellsworth Air Force Base. This facility would be used to instruct the Air Force teams on how to work on the operational sites.

As usual, they could not give Ray an exact date which kept us hanging in limbo. However, knowing that it would be soon, we drug out the moving boxes, which we saved religiously, and I began to pack. Every night when Ray got home my first question would be, "Do you know when we're leaving?" After a week of this, my very patient husband finally snapped, "No, but you'll be the first to know!" During this waiting period, Sue had a coffee party as a send-off for me. The party had just gotten a good start when Ray tracked me down, "We're leaving tonight." I put down my cup, rushed out the door and literally flew into action.

Anticipating the move, I had the trailer cleaned and ready for inspection, so all (all?) I had to do was finish up the packing, load the U Haul, corral the kids and be ready to leave as soon as Ray got home. Rain was in the forecast and Ray had reasoned that if we left that evening, we'd have a good chance of missing it. As we pulled out of the trailer court, a few raindrops fell on the windshield, raising my antenna. The further we drove, the harder the rain and the slicker the road. White-knuckled, my hands literally froze on the steering wheel and the kids, eerily quiet, no longer complained that one of them was hogging the seat. The freezing rain kept falling, the highway got worse and Ray, who was in the lead, kept driving. By now it was dark and we'd been on the road two hours which seemed like two days and I had made up my mind that I was not driving another mile! The Lord was on my side as just then, I could faintly see the lights of a town. Mental telepathy must have kicked in (no cell phones) as Ray pulled over. We stayed the night! The next morning the sun shone and the road improved, the kids once again fought for their squatters' rights, and all was back to normal.

We arrived at our destination with Christmas one week away. Being young and full of energy, I unpacked, wrote and sent out Christmas cards, trimmed the tree and baked the traditional Christmas cookies and all before Santa arrived. Plus, we planned a New Year's Eve party! Ray invited guys from work and among them was Norm Wagner who brought his wife Mary Lu. (She remembers how impressed she was with my homemade buns.) It was the beginning of a great friendship and many Bridge games, as she and Norm also settled in Derby.

It was that Christmas when I heard, via Christmas cards, that my good friend Kathy Steen in Minot was expecting a child as was our Boeing

Slim & Rose Wilderom

Turkish friend Rose Wilderom, who was ecstatic as this would be she and her husband Slim's first child. (Turned out that Bedri was their only child, which made him extra special.) It had been three years since Jeff (our youngest) was born and hearing their news, I felt a twinge of envy. Had I known what I did a couple weeks later, I could have announced the same news in our Christmas letter. Our fourth son Jim was born that next October.

Back to Grand Forks AFB

Ray's job on the Minuteman Trainer, as it was called, only lasted three months, and then it was back to Grand Forks Air Base. As luck would have it, we got the same Magnolia trailer. When we drove up to it, there was a giant sign on the door, "Welcome back. Coffee at Sue's at 10:00." We were back home. Back home and pregnant, much to the surprise of our friends...and to us.

I was happy to get our Magnolia back as it was one of the best in the court. The park manager had lived in it, and he had made some improvements to it. One was the bar between the kitchen and living room. He took the plywood off the living room side and added two shelves which he lined with a brick-patterned contact paper. I was so proud. You would have thought that I had a brand-new oak bookcase. I was the envy of all my fellow trailer friends. (Another thing we still laugh about today.)

Cheyenne, Wyoming

In June, we took out those trusty packing boxes once again. We left my fancy book case and moved to Cheyenne, Wyoming where Ray would put in another trainer. This pregnancy was very different, and it was harder to do the moving. The worst thing was the fact that I was always sleepy. I never took naps, never, and with this pregnancy, I could lie down any time of the day and sleep. This wouldn't have been so bad but I had to drive the car as Ray had the U Haul with those packed moving boxes and I had the boys. I'd get so sleepy that I would start to nod off and then I'd have to pull over and walk around the car a couple times. It was very dangerous and very foolish, but somehow, I made it. (My family has always had good guardian angels.)

As there were so few of us on this stay in Cheyenne, Boeing didn't set up a trailer court. Therefore, so we rented a cute little house. One of the first things I discovered after we moved in was that the dryer wouldn't work. I had thrown in my first load of clothes, pushed the buttons, and nothing happened. It was completely dead. I called our elderly land lord, who lived next door, and he came right over. He was as puzzled as I was as it was a fairly new dryer and the last tenants hadn't complained. It didn't take long for him to find the problem. The lint trap was packed so tightly that he had to use a tool to pry out the fuzz. When I apologized for bothering him for such a small thing, he assured me that it was no problem and to call anytime. As it turned out, they became our friends, and it was hard to leave them when we moved on.

Cheyenne, named after the Cheyenne Indians, is noted for its annual Frontier Days, an outdoor rodeo and western celebration. For the entire last week in July, the city is overrun with happy, crazy, partying people from all over and Cheyenne welcomes them with open arms. The bars and restaurants can't accommodate all of them so they spill out into the streets with their drinks in hand.

The rodeo, which is the main event, is known as "The Grand Daddy of Them All" and claims to be the world's largest outdoor rodeo. It draws top professionals who compete for more than $1 million in cash and prizes. The folks enjoyed the thrill of seeing horse and cowboy teamwork, challenging and daring feats, and tests of the true grit that it required to tame the Wild West.

Jim, Jeff. Jack, and Mike Messer

Keeping their history alive, they set up a Native American Indian village and an old frontier town with an authentic saloon. They have a chuckwagon cook-off and a free pancake breakfast three mornings a week at 7a.m. cooked and served by "chuckwagon cooks". I remember standing in line while our plates were filled and then sitting on hay bales to eat. The morning we were there, an old cowboy was playing songs on a harmonica. The boys were intrigued. In the evenings, they had top name entertainment in the grandstand. One night we saw a young Roy Clark. At the end of his show, he announced that if anyone wanted a CD, there was a '58 Rambler in the parking lot with its trunk open. It was just the beginning...

Jack celebrated his 6th birthday there in Cheyenne during Frontier Days. He was out riding his new birthday bike and took a spill on a gravel road. His knees took the brunt of it, and he had some pretty good chunks of gravel in them. Ray cleaned them up but couldn't get one large piece out. Jack hopped down from the table, got a butcher knife, and told his dad, "Try this." We were off to the emergency room. Frontier Days truly exemplifies the old Wild, and it keeps the emergency rooms busy. That evening was no different. A cowboy, possibly one of the bull riders, looked like he'd been in a good fight and came out the loser. His one eye was swollen shut, his face all scratched, and he seemed to be holding his ribs. Jack was all eyes and asked, "Did he fall off his bike, too?" And then there was the woman, reeking of stale cigarette smoke and booze, who stuck out her hand to the admission person and told her that she'd been bitten. The nurse must have asked what kind of bite as we couldn't help but hear her answer, "Human!" We could still hear her muttering as she disappeared down the hall.

Finally, Jack's name was called. The doctor who saw him explained that he was an anesthesiologist. He had been called in to be a standby for a doctor who was replacing a battery in a pace maker. Jack had been listening intently and when the doctor started to "fix" his knee, he asked, "Are you sure you know what you're doing?" The doctor laughed and said that he had twin boys and he's done this same thing at home on the kitchen table many times. Satisfied, our brave little guy laid back and never even flinched when the doctor removed the stone. Yes, it was quite the experience that night in the emergency room during the infamous Frontier Days in Cheyenne, WY.

Return to Minot, North Dakota

In August of '68, we once again packed those large boxes, and headed to North Dakota, and for the first time we moved into our house on 17 acres in Foxholm right next door to the house I was raised in and where my mother still lived. Ray worked at the Minot Air Base (just 12 miles over the hill from Foxholm) in Electronic Test and Maintenance (ETM). His crews repaired and tested electronic equipment for Boeing Assembling and Checkout crews in the field. This was the fourth and last move we made while I was pregnant with Jim. He was born that October in St. Joseph Hospital in Minot, the same hospital I was born in.

The week after Thanksgiving, Ray was transferred to Sedalia, Missouri to take over the ETM shop. We decided that because the baby was so young, the boys and I would stay in Foxholm until Christmas when Ray would come back to move us. He did come back, as planned, but I had gotten the flu and was too sick to move. I was left in North Dakota with three little boys and a new baby in the dead of the winter. My family and friends came to my rescue. Someone would check on me daily, and then little Jack was such a good help with the baby. Slowly I regained my strength. I would be ready to move as soon as Ray came for us.

It's a good thing that I was in home territory as I was met with many challenges, which can be described in one word-WINTER. And was it ever winter, a winter filled with bitterly cold temperatures, blizzards and more blizzards. There were massive snow banks in the yard, and our driveway was continually blocked. Adam Keller, who lived in town, worked for the county and had access to a mighty snow removal machine. He would plow out the drive one day, and the next day it would be all filled in, again! Luckily, Mike and Jack rode a school bus that went right past our house so I didn't have that worry. Getting groceries and going to church on Sundays was another thing. Again, friends and family came to my rescue. Art and Lois Rademacher would grocery shop for me when they went to Minot and then drop them off on the road in front of our house, and my mother and I would alternate going to Mass. One Sunday, she would climb over the snow banks between our two houses and take care of the baby while the boys and I hooked a ride to church. The next Sunday she'd go to church. Luckily, Jim was a good baby and never got sick, didn't even have a cold until he was over a year old.

Mike had his ninth birthday in January, in the very heart of this frigid snowy winter. I wanted to do something to celebrate but it was impossible to go anywhere with all the snow, and his school friends couldn't come for a party. So,

I baked and decorated him a cake, made a special dinner and invited the two little Larson boys who lived across the highway from us. I watched as they climbed over and through the snow drifts and then called their mom to tell her that they made it! I had to laugh when they came into the house. Their cheeks and noses were cherry red from the cold, and snow clung to their snowsuits and stocking caps, making them look like two fat little snowmen. They played awhile, had dinner and then we sang "Happy Birthday" as Mike blew out the candles. After gigantic pieces of chocolate cake, it was time for them to put on those snowsuits and tackle the snow drifts once again. This time Madeline called when they got back home. It was a different kind of birthday party, but it was a party and Mike went to bed happy, and that's what it was all about.

And then one day, I got a call from a high school friend. Would I play a charity game of basketball with "the old folks" against the current high school girls' team? I had played basketball all during high school and thought it sounded like fun. Mom volunteered to come over and take care of the boys. I dug out my basketball shoes and was on my way! We didn't win, but we gave them a run for their money, and I was given an honorary award for being "The Only Nursing Mother on The Court". When I got home, Mom was sitting on the couch and Jack was rocking a sleeping baby. Little Jimmy had cried and cried and nothing his grandmother did would soothe him. Finally, Jack said, "Here let me try." The crying stopped and soon the baby was sound asleep in his brother's arms.

Grand Forks AFB, North Dakota

Ray did come back as promised. We didn't leave immediately, however, as he had volunteered for a temporary two-week assignment at Minot Air Force Base to assist the Corp of Engineers, Boeing, and Air Force SATF to kit-proof the modification of the standby diesel generators. At the end of those two weeks, we loaded up those packing boxes and left for Sedalia, this time with family intact. Once again, it was a Magnolia trailer for us but this time we kept the packing boxes within reach as it was to be a short stay (another one!) as Ray had to go back to the Grand Forks Air Base.

 There was no housing in Grand Forks this time, so we found a place in the little town of Larimore, 30 miles west of Grand Forks, and Ray drove 10 miles back and forth to the base every day. This move was hard for me. We were the only Boeing people living there, and I was used to living among friends and family, and I didn't know a soul. We lived in a four-plex, so one would think that at least one person would be friendly. Wrong, not even one! I was so lonesome. I remember walking down-town with the baby to a store that sold dry goods. I bought some material, and the sales lady actually visited with me. After meeting her, I found that I "needed" a little more fabric, and then it was thread and stick pins, and so I survived.

We all remember one milestone while there-Jim learned to walk. We were in the living room watching the first time a man walked on the moon. It was July 20, 1969. Just as Neil Armstrong stepped out of the Lunar Lander, Jim pulled himself up and literally ran across the room, slapped the television (our 39-inch black and white), turned around, and gave us a big smile, as if to say, "I did it!" He was a few days past nine months old.

Boeing was cutting down on staff at this time, and Ray was one of the men they surplused. Dick Holly, a friend who worked in Boeing personnel, found Ray a Fort Worth-based position on the AGM (Air to Ground SRAM Missile) program. By Gross, the one who laid off Ray, didn't realize that Ray was the last Boeing man certified for the nuclear two-man team on the base. (A nuclear two-man team was required to be there whenever people were below ground in the missile facility. This was designed to prevent accidental or malicious launch of nuclear weapons by a single individual.) When Gross discovered his error, he immediately tried to cancel the surplus. Without further discussion, Holly told him, "Tough! Messer is going to Fort Worth." Out came those boxes (this time happily), and the Messers headed south.

Fort Worth, Texas

Usually when we moved, we had only to locate the Boeing Trailer Court. This, however, was a different situation. There was no one waiting to greet us with supper on the table and the latest Boeing news. We were on our own in this huge city.

Luckily, there was one Boeing family there, Virg and Dorothy Miller, who graciously offered to put us up while house hunting. Virg and Dorothy were also NoDakers, Virg actually grew up in Minot, so that helped us feel less like interlopers in our new city.

Virg was an outstanding athlete who participated in many sports during his high school and college years. Virg's father had also been a notable athlete in his day, and his continued participation in Minot's sports-world earned him the honor of having a sports complex named after him. And yet, Virg told us, with tears in his eyes, that his dad had never attended one of his games. He talked about the dads clustering around after a game, waiting to praise their sons as they came out of the locker room. "But", Virg said sadly, "My dad was never one of them."

We found a house to rent in a record five days. It was a three bedroom, plus an enclosed sun porch off the kitchen, which I considered an added bonus. I could visualize a cozy little nook flanked with green plants where I could hide away and relax with a good book.

Moving day was, as usual, another sweltering hot Texas summer day. While in the garage, Ray saw that the cover on the attic was open. He automatically reached up and closed it. As we unloaded our boxes, we noticed an odor that smelled suspiciously like cat pee. The hotter the day became, the stronger the odor. Then we began to hear strange sounds that seemed to be coming from the attic. Cautiously, Ray opened the trap door. A large Tom cat and at least five of his girlfriends shot out, just missing Ray's head! The stench was unbelievable!

The kitchen was my first project. I found the box marked "dishes" and carefully removed them from the towels I had packed them in. As I opened the cupboard door, I smelled a faint familiar odor. Cat pee? My first thought was, "It can't be. In the cupboard?" In the cupboard! Later, a neighbor told me that the people who lived there before us had cats that routinely walked on the cupboards, and once, she actually saw one climbing into it. I took the dishes back out rewashed them all. (It was evident that the sink in our master bathroom had also been a favorite spot for their cats!)

The sunroom, with all its glass, led to the back yard, and every time I walked through, a now very familiar odor jumped up and hit me. Curious, I gingerly pulled up the old carpet. The concrete floor under it was covered with urine stains! The answer was clear, the reflected heat from the sliding glass door had literally baked in the acrid smell. The rug was out in the backyard in minutes, and I was back to scrubbing, really scrubbing this time.

Ray called the landlord several times, but each time he was given the run-around. Finally, my usually very patient husband rolled up the foul carpet, and threw it in the trunk of our car. The next morning, after moldering in the closed trunk overnight, he delivered it to our landlord at his service station. When the trunk was opened, steaming stench rolled out in waves nearly knocking over a startled man at the gas pump. Ray walked up to the front door of the station, threw down the rug, turned around and left. He could keep his carpet.

Our neighbors had a big German Sheppard in their backyard, that was strictly a guard dog, not a pet. He did his job so well that I couldn't wash the windows on that side of the house. As soon as I came around the corner, he would lunge at me with teeth barred. Little 8-yr. old Jack to the rescue! It hadn't taken him a day to make friends with Max, and consequently, he became the window washer. Then came the day when I looked out the patio door to see our year-old Jimmy toddle up to the fence and stick his hand through. My heart nearly stopped. Before I could even move, Max was right there. He gave Jimmy's little hand a good lick, wagged his tail, and slowly sauntered back to his dog house. The power of little children. Eventually, Max and I also became friends. I had a fool-proof method; I threw pieces of meat over the fence. (Works every time!)

Just as we were nicely settled in, our air conditioner gave one last shutter and died. We never had one breath of cool air for six long weeks, in spite of our many calls to, and promises from, our great landlord. (Great landlord who, we figured out, was broke, but now did have an extra carpet.) During these weeks of roasting, we survived by spending our days swimming at General Dynamics recreational area. Ray was working nights, which left the kids and I alone in our remarkably hot house in that big city, and I was afraid to leave the windows open. We suffocated. And then I thought of Max; he would protect us. The windows were opened.

After the air conditioner fiasco, we spent the rest of our time on Bandera Drive quite happily. Dora Sloan lived near-by, and we became fast friends, as did her son Chad and Jeff. She also had a beautiful little red-headed girl named Melissa,

46

who became a famous hair stylist, and worked on the elite of Fort Worth. Dora made Fort Worth for me. I turned to her many times to share good news and the not so good. When we moved, it was very hard leaving her, and I vowed to never, again, let myself become that close to someone who I knew I'd have to leave. I did break that vow but, it was never as hard leaving as it was when I left Dora. We remained long-distance friends until she passed away in 2018.

After a year, we moved just two blocks away to Pinto Trail. When we left, we said good-bye to Max only. (We had never met his elusive owners.) Our new home had air conditioning, and no cats! What it did have was filth. The previous tenants had run a catering business from their home and what I found made me wonder if they had ever been inspected. When I was down on my hands and knees scrubbing the kitchen floor, I discovered that what I had thought was quarter-round that lined the walls was actually a build-up of grease and dirt. I have never been as tired as I was when I went to bed that night. Never! (I often wondered if our landlord realized what a good deal he got when we moved in.)

With school starting, the kids and I looked for the best route for them to walk to school. The first street we walked on was Las Vegas Trail, a bustling street, and I quickly ruled that one out. After a little more scouting, we found a much safer way. During the first week, Mike, a fifth-grader, was chosen to be a crossing guard. On his first day on duty, I was shocked to see him come storming into the house with his little brother Jimmy in tow, "Mom, do you know where I found this kid?" That kid had climbed our four-foot chain link fence in the back yard and was walking on Las Vegas Blvd., almost to Waverly Park school when Mike spotted him. I was shocked! Never had I thought that someone so little could get out of a yard that was surrounded by a fence that high. Little did I know that he would become adept at many things that I thought would never be possible.

We had another adventurous son. Jack was always out exploring. We lived on the edge of Fort Worth, and there were hills and little streams near-by. They drew him like a magnet. Once he set out on his wonderings, he forgot all our warnings. Ray and I were forever looking for him. He'd go one way, and I the other. We actually had our signal-whoever found him first would turn on the front porch light. One day the mailman brought him home, and before I could say anything, he assured me that head wounds looked worse than they were. Jack's head and face was covered with blood that ran down his cheeks and soaked into his tee shirt. He had gotten in the way of a rock, that was thrown by a playmate. The mailman was right. After I got him cleaned up, all he needed were a couple of band-aids that I bought by the gross. Interesting how those childhood traits follow them into adulthood.

Mike received a high-honors award for being the outstanding student of the year at Waverly Park, and his plaque was hung in the hallway along with the previous award winners. And Jeff earned an award from Miss Lu Nell Barnett, his young redheaded sweet kindergarten teacher for achieving his goal of learning how to count to ten in Spanish.

Mike and Jack were on a little league baseball team, and we spent many summer evenings going to ball games. An annual event on that league was for the mothers of one team to play the mothers of another team. Naturally, I was the first in line to sign up! During practice, one of the mothers, who had previously played in this event, warned me that one certain mother was very aggressive and would knock the baseman off the bag, if she had to. I was playing third and what she didn't know was that I was just as determined to stay on the bag! Sure enough, she came barreling into third and I was ready for her, with ball in hand, to make the out! I stuck out my arm, and she was on the ground, out cold. I don't remember who won the game, but I do vividly remember that play! (She probably does, too.)

Fort Worth was a huge metropolis, especially to those who were born and raised in towns so small that if you met three cars on the street, it was a traffic jam. Therefore, you'll understand my surprise when I first went grocery shopping. Instead of changing banks whenever we moved, we kept our North Dakota bank. Knowing I'd have to have it approved, I went directly to the window. When the woman looked at the check, her eyes immediately lit up. "North Dakota, I lived on the Minot Air Base." Of course, I told her that I was from the little town of Foxholm, which was just 12 miles from that base. "Oh," she said excitedly, "did you know Ma Miller?" Imagine my surprise! Imagine her surprise when I told her that she was my mother! She and her husband used to go fishing in Lake Darling, which is near Foxholm, and would stop at Mom's bar where she sold them beer and minnows, laced with genuine old-fashioned friendship. It is, indeed, a very small world.

We made an attempt to attend the State Fair in every state that we lived. In Texas, the fair was in Dallas. Being fairly close, we drove down on a Saturday afternoon. We parked in one of the huge parking lots, took our ticket from the attendant, and entered The State Fair Park. We immediately sensed a difference from all the others, we had attended. The Texas State Fair had a definite urban feeling to it. As we strolled through all the rides and concessions, it didn't take long before noticing that police in groups of three constantly patrolled the grounds, something we had never seen before.

The afternoon faded into evening, and there was one more attraction that the bigger boys insisted on going through-the Spook House. I decided to stay back with little Jim and Jeff. As we stood there waiting, I was suddenly aware of jostling behind us, and then I felt someone push into me. I turned and saw the flash of knives. Two big, tough-looking guys were in a vicious knife fight right beside us! In a matter of seconds, three policemen were on them! It had happened so quickly that we didn't have time to even react until later, when it all soaked in. We missed the Spook House but we had had our own scare, and it was the real thing!

It didn't take long to decide that we had enough of the fair. We cautiously wove our way through the throng of people, found the exit, and left. The parking lot was poorly lit, and we couldn't find our car. We walked up and down, and no car. Finally, we saw a cop, who was patrolling the area. We flagged him down, showed him our parking stub, and asked if he could help us. He took a brief look, said he wasn't familiar with the parking lots, and he couldn't help us. By now, it was really dark, and spooky! There we stood, in the middle of that big parking lot in Dallas, and not knowing where to go or what to do next. I was beyond the panic stage. And then, our ten-year old son Mike said, "Dad, we didn't go in this gate." Sure enough, we had left through the wrong gate and were in the wrong parking lot. We re-entered, left through the correct exit and hallelujah, there it was, our car, right where we'd left it!

We became good friends with those who worked with Ray and got together often. Dave and Louise Stover were one of the couples. I remember spending Thanksgiving at their house, and the reason I remember is because it was the first, and last, time we had smoked turkey instead of roast turkey and dressing for Thanksgiving dinner.

One of our outings was to The Windmill Dinner theater in Dallas. Boots Randolph, Chet Adkins and Floyd Kramer performed. It was our kind of music and when Boots played that sax, I was once again seventeen, and on my Senior Class Skip Day in Minneapolis, dancing the night away in the Prom Ball Room to the music of Frankie Carl and His Orchestra. With all that good music, and it being our first dinner theater, it was a night to remember.

Many times, on a Saturday, we would make the trip downtown to Leonard's Department store, whose corporation was the founder of Radio Shack. Leonard's, started by two farm boys with ingenuity, determination and 600 dollars, was as big as a suburban mall (before we knew what an urban shopping center is) and was as well stocked as an urban shopping center. And it was all in a single store downtown, when we still shopped downtown. It was a vast three-story building with a parking lot so big that they ran a train from the parking lot into the store's lower level. The boys loved the train and it was one of the reasons they liked to go to Leonard's.

Leonard's called itself a "one-stop shopping center" and it was hard to argue with that boast. It sold anything you could imagine- pianos, petticoats, pumpkin seeds, wave set, lawn mowers lubricated by Leonard's brand of motor oil, shoes (Ray bought the boys' boots there.), groceries, glass wear, candy that they made right in front of the customers and bakery goods that were baked in their own ovens. Delicious odors wafted through the store and invariably we went home with a bag full of donuts.

The Leonard brothers were masters of promotion. We remember one promotional sale on some name-brand trousers. They were advertised as any size, and any color (as long as it was yellow), and they were only $2.00 a pair! When we walked into the store, we were bombarded by a sea of yellow! Every salesman, and there were many, had on yellow pants! We knew the sale had to have been a success (Ray even bought a pair) as, every once in a while, when we were out and about, we saw those yellow pants walk by.

The Leonards were early movers and shakers in the Ft. Worth area. Marvin Leonard ("Mr. Marvin" as everyone called him), was an avid golfer. He founded the Colonial Country Club and Golf Course in 1946 and started the National Invitation Tournament. He was a close friend and sponsor of Ben Hogan, one of golf's greatest.

While in FT. Worth, Ray and my anniversary happened to fall during the Colonial Golf tournament. We celebrated by going out for dinner at the Farmer's Daughter restaurant, which was the place to go at that time. Seated at the next table were Lee Trivino, Merle Blancas and Gene Littler. (Blancas won the tournament that year.) We wanted to jump up and ask for their autographs, but we nonchalantly kept eating, and listening, and stealing glances. That was the closest we've ever come to the infamous Colonial Golf tournament.

Time marches on and Leonard's Empire is a thing of the past. The only thing remaining are memories and our memories of Leonard's are some of our best.

50

Minot, North Dakota

In August 1971, Ray's Boeing job at GD was completed and it was on the road again for the Messers. Ray took us back to Minot early so the boys could start school. He helped us find a house, unloaded the U-Haul and returned to Fort Worth to finish up his job.

It didn't take long to discover that this house was not the one for us. Newly-weds were living in the basement apartment, and the acoustics were excellent. With young boys, it was not an ideal situation, to say the least. Luckily, I heard of a little house that was for rent on 11th Ave. N.W., which was owned by the notable attorney, Ella Van Berkom. (It was rumored that if you were guilty, you hired Ella. Interestingly, Ella had never gone to law school. She had worked in a law office, where she soaked up enough knowledge to pass the bar exams.) Five days after I had unpacked those notorious boxes, I pulled them back out and with my sister Evie's help, we repacked everything, and were off to the "little green house", as we called it.

Four weeks after Ray returned to Fort Worth, his job was finished and, once again, he loaded the remaining things into a U-Haul trailer (The vacuum cleaner was always the last to be loaded.) and was on his way to join us. (Some years later, Lou and Kathy Pariso's little girl Cindy said, as they passed a U-Haul truck on the highway, "There's some Boeing people.")

He stopped on his way out of town to fill up with gas and overheard the owner talking to a crusty, old, tobacco-chewing cowboy, who obviously was a long-time friend. The owner asked about the troublesome "wet backs" the rancher had hired. "Problem solved," the old man answered, "They're in the stock pond."

As Ray was driving north, the big news on the radio was about the four immigrants from Mexico, who were killed in a poolroom brawl in Ft. Worth. And when he hit the North Dakota border, the big news on the radio was, "A 19 yr. old AWOL soldier has been apprehended in a motel in Dickinson." That was in 1971. Today, due to the oil industry, things in North Dakota have changed considerably.

Ray found a job in Minot building aircraft doors for Lockheed's L-1011. After working for two months, Dick Holly, who was in IR (Industrial Relations) with Boeing, tracked Ray down, and offered him a job in Rapid City, South Dakota where he would work in ETM (Electronic Test and Maintenance). This was in

October, 1971. When Dick Holly was in Minot, he met and married Mary Ann. (Some years before they met, her husband had taken their three children to Baker's Bridge on the Souris River near Foxholm, drowned them, and then took his own life.)

Since the boys were settled in school, we decided that Ray would leave, and come back to move us after Christmas.

Rapid City, South Dakota

Ray rented a motel room and went house-hunting. He found one that needed a good paint job, and a little cleaning, but otherwise would be just the one for us. It was near a school and a grocery store, and it had a good view of the beautiful Black Hills. Since Ray was alone with nothing to do on weekends, it seemed like the perfect deal. He signed the contract and the landlord bought the paint! From then on, every time I talked to Ray, I would eagerly ask him how the painting was going. Each time he assured me that it was coming along. I asked him so many times that finally he snapped at me," It's coming along fine!" Knowing my husband, who would rather read than eat, I had an uneasy feeling.

Christmas came, and Ray arrived on time to celebrate with us. After the holidays, we loaded those well-used boxes, which I had packed and ready to go, into a U-Haul trailer. I said good-bye to my family and to Kathy Steen, my good friend, who had thought we were finally living in the same city, and down the road we went.

Ray led in the U-Haul, and I followed in the car with the boys, and constantly heard, "He's touching me!" or "He's on my side." or I'm hungry." Having no cell phones, we relied on mental telepathy when we were hungry or needed a potty break and, most of the time, the telepathy didn't work.

And so, it went until we finally arrived in Rapid City-tired, hungry and with what seemed like twelve kids. I was so grateful that we had a house all ready for us. When we walked in, I wanted to turn around, walk right back out, and head for the nearest lawyer! My husband, who had assured me all those times, had not finished the painting! Feeling sorry for myself, I spent the evening in tears. Finally, Jack said to me, "Don't worry, Mom, you'll make it into a home for us." And yes, once again, it did become our home.

We unloaded and I enrolled the boys in their new school. I finished the painting, we were still married, and for a little while things settled down. Mike who always loved school was not happy in his new one. He finally told me why. He was being harassed by a group of kids. When Ray and I went to the principal, we found out that the harassment was master-minded by a group of very mean girls. It wasn't their first offense, nor was it their second. We found they had a history of violence and ended up being kicked out of that school, forever.

While we were there, Little Jimmy and Jeff somehow contracted oral herpes which covered the insides of their mouth and throat with painful sores. They couldn't eat or drink for days, especially Jimmy, who was just three. No matter what we tried to give him, he refused. He grew listless and weak. Finally, we thought we'd have to take him into the emergency room as we worried about dehydration. Trying one more time, Ray offered him the 7-Up which he had refused repeatedly. To our surprise, he took the bottle and drank almost half of it. From then on, it was all up-hill and he soon became his happy little animated self.

My brother Ralph and his wife Edith, who owned and operated the Speedway Bar near Minot, usually found us where ever we were living, Rapid City included. While eating dinner one evening, Jimmy, who was sitting next to his uncle, was liberally buttering his bun. Ralph looked over and said, "You've got an awful lot of butter there, don't you?" and without missing a beat, Jimmy answered, "Well, I've got an awful lot of bun."

As more Boeing people arrived, a Boeing trailer park was set up. We put our furniture into storage and moved into another Magnolia trailer. We were happy as we all had friends there, plus, our rent was a whole lot cheaper.

54

The Rapid City Flood of 1972

Only days after we moved into the trailer court, we had to make a trip to Minot to take care of some flood damage that was done to our house in Foxholm. I had everything ready to go when Ray got home from work and in a matter of minutes, we were on the road. We stopped in Sturgis to pick up some take-out chicken for dinner. As we drove out of town, it started to rain. Fortunately, we drove out of it and reached Minot late that evening.

That next morning, we were having breakfast at my sister Connie's when her phone rang. It was her friend Fran who anxiously asked, "How are Ray and Myrna?" Surprised at the question, Connie told her that we were fine, and, as a matter of fact, we were right there at her table. "Have you seen the news," she asked? We turned on the TV and were stunned at what we heard, "Rapid City, South Dakota devastated by a flash flood...failure of the dam at Canyon Lake." And there, as big as life, were mobile homes bobbing up and down... in our trailer park! Immediately, Ray called Ray Bitel and asked him what he knew about the flood. "What flood?" he answered. Ray and Sue didn't live in our trailer court. They had rented a house in a hilly section of town. Sue's parents were there visiting, and they had driven up into the hills that afternoon to do some sight-seeing. Sue remembers that it had rained hard until they got back into Rapid. That night they had gone out to a night club, The Imperial 500 (a club we also frequented), where they danced the night away, oblivious to what was happening around them. It was raining when they left around midnight but they had no idea that on the other side of the town, it was pouring down and flooding. They still didn't know in the morning, even when Scott and Shelley with their cereal bowls in hand, complained that the television wouldn't work and they couldn't watch cartoons.

We immediately returned to Rapid City, and were horrified at what we saw. Devastation from the flood was everywhere. When we got to our trailer court, we couldn't believe our eyes. Our trailer was still standing, but three trailers down from us, everything was gone. Completely washed away!

Mary Lu and Norm Wagner lived two trailers from us. Their station wagon had floated away, but their boat stayed. They, too, had left Friday after work. They were taking Norm's mother home to Washington and had stopped for gas on Saturday morning in Ennis, Montana. Seeing the South Dakota license plate, the attendant said, "Quite the flood they had there." Surprised, Norm questioned,

"What flood?" He quickly found a newspaper, and sure enough! He tried to call his friend Duane Lund, but all the lines were down. He finally called the Boeing operator in Seattle. They contacted the Air Force Base in Rapid who plugged him in with the Lunds. They did go on to Seattle but turned right around and headed back to South Dakota.

Water had covered the floor of our trailer, but most of our things were intact. Since we had recently moved, we still had some things in the truck and in our storage unit beside our trailer. Before we left, Ray had backed the truck up against the storage unit to secure both of them. When all the water poured in, the shed broke its force, and thus there was no damage to the truck. We did lose most of the stuff in the storage unit, including all Ray's slides from his army days in Alaska and our photos. We salvaged the black and white ones as we could wash off the mud, but the colored pictures were ruined. Yet, we considered ourselves very lucky.

The Rapid City flood was the most detrimental flood in South Dakota's history and one of the deadliest floods in United States history. Two hundred and thirty-eight people lost their lives, and the property damage was estimated to be over 160 million. (Would be 990 million in 2021 dollars.)

On that Friday in July, there had been 16 inches of rain up in the mountains, which caused the Rapid Creek to overflow. The run-off carried rubble down to the Canyon Lake Dam, causing it to break, flooding everything in its wake. The result was totally unbelievable. When the sun rose the next morning, a large house was sitting in the middle of Jackson Boulevard, one of the main city streets. It had floated all the way down the canyon, accompanied by several large uprooted trees, and came to rest in front of Bacon Park shopping center. It looked like it had been carefully picked up and placed there. Every direction one looked you could see destruction. The cars at the auto dealerships were jumbled up in a pile. All these years later, I can still see them. They reminded me of flattened tin cans stacked up against one another. Light poles were ripped up and scattered across the streets like children's pick-up-sticks. The flood tore houses from their foundations. Old stately trees were yanked from the ground with their long-thick roots now lying limply on top of the sodden earth. A trailer park, only a couple blocks from us, was utterly swept away, leaving not a single trace of all that had been there only hours before.

57

There were so many tragic stories of people who suffered through the flood. Many sat on the roofs of their houses and watched in horror as the swirling, angry water rose higher and higher. Flashes of lightning revealed people clinging in trees, their cries for help swallowed by the roar of the water. A grandmother stood for hours in shoulder-high water, holding her adult handicapped granddaughter afloat on a mattress. One young man rode for miles down Rapid Creek, clinging to a propane tank. The survivors called it a nightmare that was never forgotten.

And to bring it closer to home, a Boeing friend of ours was out walking with her young son that next morning when he spotted, what he thought was a softball that was unraveling, lying among all the debris. When he bent down to pick it up, he discovered that it was a woman's head, grotesquely sticking out from under some twisted boards that covered her body. It took a long time, and many therapy sessions, for Craig to be able to go anywhere without his mother by his side.

Ray's good high school buddy Larry Vail, who worked for West River Electric was out in the storm doing service calls when he and his co-worker were caught in a sudden rush of water, which nearly covered their truck. They somehow crawled to the top of their vehicle, where they lay for hours with the black water inching upward. As they strained to see through the heavy rain, they saw several large mobile homes from a near-by trailer court floating towards them. The lead mobile home suddenly slid sideways, blocking the road for those behind and thus preventing them from crashing into the West River truck. Larry and his co-worker remained clinging to the truck with water nearly touching them. Had it not been for the spot light on the utility truck that was still shinning, they would never have been seen and rescued. Later Larry quipped, "That Sears Die Hard battery (which had powered the spot-light while under water) sure lived up to its name." Boeing workers joined in to help clean up the mess and search for the survivors. They stumbled over concrete foundations and partial stairways as they cleared mud from the streets and buildings. They hauled away tons of smashed vehicles and mounds of debris. One group helping to untangle the bleachers on the School of Mines football field found two people crushed under a pile of splintered wood. They also hauled water which had to be boiled before using, and everyone was required to have a typhoid shot.

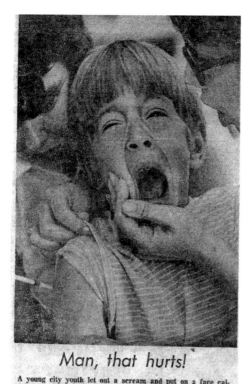

Man, that hurts!

A young city youth let out a scream and put on a face calculated to earn an Academy Award Tuesday as he received a typhoid shot at a first aid station. Most of the people in and around Rapid City were getting the shots. (AP Wirephoto)

A photographer for a national news service caught our eight-year-old son Jeff just as the needle went into his arm. His terrified scream was "heard" via the Associated Press' wire photo all over the country. A friend told us he saw it in Seattle and another saw it in Minnesota.

Exactly one week later, just as we were just sitting down for dinner, the siren went off. Immediately, we were out the door, and into pouring down rain. The water was already to the bottom of the car door as we inched our way to the park exit, which was clogged with cars and trucks. As we slowly moved, I looked over, and saw our neighbor, with her kids in their station wagon, stalled at the entrance. (Her husband had taken their truck.) She had run out of gas. I couldn't believe it! No way in hell would I have been separated from Ray, no matter how many vehicles we lost. When we finally made it to the street, we headed south towards the overpass. The water was rising fast, and we had to turn around twice. I was frantic. I had visions of Jimmy being pulled from my arms and being swept away in the raging water. (The previous week's stories were all too fresh.) Finally, with water tearing at our wheels, we made it to higher ground, the Moose Club's parking lot. There we waited in total darkness for what seemed like forever, until we were able to return home where our supper waited on the table. Later we learned that just behind our car, a young couple was swept into a drainage ditch and drowned.

Unlike the week before, there was little structural damage in the city, and although the panic level was at a record high, there were few deaths. This time, people had taken the warning seriously.

One of the better things about living in Rapid City was that Larry and Barbara Vail lived there. Larry and Ray graduated from Bowman High School in 1951. (Larry was the one rescued in the flood.) They had the best time reminiscing. I think every time they told a story, and there were many, it had gotten a little longer and more embellished. They made a good pair. Sadly, Larry passed away in 2019. We had stopped in to see them on our way to North Dakota not too long before he died. We're so happy that we did as we had such a good visit. Little did we know it would be the last time we saw him.

Larry Vail and Ray Messer

When Louie and Andy Belisle and their two kids, Steve and Connie, were moving from Great Falls to Rapid City, a wheel on their trailer broke off and flew across the road at great speed. It was eleven at night. They hadn't stopped to eat, they were tired from driving all day, and there they were, minus one wheel, somewhere in Montana in the middle of the night. Louie got out and searched blindly in the ditch full of weeds. He found nothing. While pondering their predicament, he saw a faint light in the distance and started walking. Luckily, it was a house next to a junk yard. He woke up the junk dealer, and after rummaging in the dark, they found a useable wheel and tire. Louie rolled it back to their truck and finally got it mounted, only to find that the inner tube leaked. He took the wheel off for a second time, rolled it back down the highway to the

60

junk yard and found another inner tube. He finally got the tire on the wheel, and the exhausted Belisles were back in business. They limped their way into Miles City, found a motel and went to bed hungry.

The next morning, rested and their hunger satisfied, Louie purchased a brand-new wheel, and the rejuvenated Belisles were on the road.

Andy and Louie Belisle

The Taurus Program

The Taurus Program, on which Louie worked, took place near Mission, South Dakota and also on a site near Bradly, MT. They were working on a method of testing the vulnerability of the EMP (Electric Magnetic Pulse) by simulating a nuclear bomb exploding in the air. They installed equipment to generate the pulse, all done with magnetic pulses, on a giant balloon that was filled with helium, a balloon so large that it took four days for the country to produce enough helium to fill it. Their idea was to raise up the balloon carrying the equipment to about 100 feet so that they could test "shooting" down on the missile site.

Taurus Balloon

They planned to tether the balloon to a bulldozer which they would move to specific locations so it could "fire down at their target". (Their plans had been to move the balloon to other missile sites and do the same.)

A big facility to support the elaborate set-up was needed. They moved in a dozeor more trailers, including one which held a colossal diesel power generator. Others were used to house equipment, several offices, and even a food trailer.

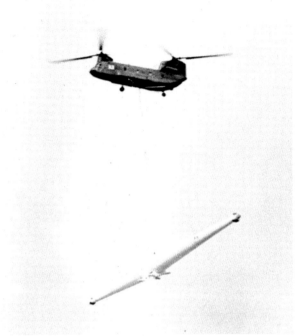

CH- 47 chopper handling Tauras probe

Probe being unloaded from aircraft

It was winter and to prove it, a powerful blizzard tore through the area. There was only one guard, Carlin Miller (a barber from Sturgis) on the launch site when it hit. It took out 25 power poles which cut off all commercial power to the site leaving Carlin in the dark, with no heat, in the middle of a raging blizzard. All the roads were blocked solid, and the weatherman said, "Absolutely no travel." Yet Boeing had not called off work.

Blizzard during The Taurus Program in Mission, South Dakota

Andy Androwski and a crew were sent out to the site to rescue the guard. They got as far as Sturgis. It was impossible to go another foot, and the guard was still without heat or lights, in below-zero temperatures during a raging blizzard! The only means of communicate was by radio, and Louie Belisle spent three and a half hours talking to the guard, giving him step by step instructions on how to start a gigantic generator in one of the semi's trailers. Carlin, a novice on generators, had only three tries to start it. On the third pull of the lever, it kicked in. Louie then had to guide him in the transfer of power to another trailer. He did it! He had power, and thus, lights and heat. It was days before he was rescued, and he run out of food. He rummaged through all the trailers on the site and scrounged up every scrap he could find. It was barely enough to sustain him until they were finally able to break through the enormous snow banks and free him.

The Taurus Program was a good idea but, unfortunately, it didn't work. When they tethered the balloon to the bulldozer, it was so strong that it lifted the bulldozer right off the ground. After all the time, effort, and man-power invested,

64

the testing was scratched. There would be no experimental "shooting" at any missile sites.

Louie Belisle

Blocked roads to LF site

Taurus Work Group

Cheyenne, Wyoming

That August found us dragging out the packing boxes once again. We retrieved our things that were in storage and headed out to Cheyenne, Wyoming, just in time for the Frontier Days-again.

We moved into the Boeing trailer park that was close to the Francis E Warren Air Base. (There were two Boeing Trailer courts to accommodate the 500 families who traveled with us, although not everyone moved at exactly the same time.) It was nestled in a low grassy area just down the hill from the State Capitol building, right across the Interstate from Francis E Warren Air Force Base.

We Boeing Gypsies were an eclectic group from many different walks of life who were tied together through a common cause...our kids liked to eat.

Just across the street, and up a couple of trailers, were Larry and Gale Kane and their three little girls. You couldn't find a nicer gal than Gale. She was a natural at making a person feel at home, and traveling like we did, that was an excellent trait. She had three cute little girls, (I shared my birthday with Candy.) who entertained Jim. They used to make a "fort" by covering the front steps with a blanket, where they happily played while Gale and I exchanged stories and recipes at her kitchen table.

Gale Kane

When I think of Gale, I remember a friend of hers whom I met on several occasions. She was a strikingly pretty young blond with a ten-year-old daughter from a previous marriage. Her ex-husband, the little girl's father, was a known member of a notorious mob in New York City and was shot and killed while we were in Cheyenne. Gale's friend and her young daughter were flown to New York where they were met and escorted to the funeral in an armored car. It made for good conversation at many coffee parties.

Larry remembers the time he went to cash his per diem check at Safeway, and they refused to cash it. "Insufficient funds", he was told. Larry went back to the office, and told The Head of Finance, John Biltz. It was a fast trip back to the store where Biltz told them, in no uncertain terms, "Boeing is not broke!" Larry's check was cashed with several apologies and no further hesitation, as were all his future checks. We saw Gale and Larry at our great Boeing reunion in 1999 in Laughlin, Nevada, and Gale hadn't changed a bit. It was as if we were back in her kitchen having a comfortable cup of coffee.

Barbara and Bill Hansen and their family of six were Mormons from Utah. They lived right next door to us. It was their first time out in the field away from home. They had a small baby and whenever Barbara had a concern, she'd call her doctor back in Utah. She was so nice and friendly, a wonderful neighbor, but her husband was much more reserved. Barbara and I saw each other during the day and our kids were friends, but we never socialized with them as a family.

Another couple who lived near us was J.P. and Marilyn Paulson. They had their 25th wedding anniversary while we were in Cheyenne. Jim love telling stories, and when Ray asked him how the celebration went, he said, "It was just like 25 years ago, only this time I went in the bathroom and cried." Marilyn merely raised an eyebrow. After 25 years, she was used to his humor.

Maynard and Marie Mattern were from Hatton, North Dakota. They also lived just a couple trailers from us. I knew Teresa, Marie's sister, as she and her husband Art Aarseth lived on a farm near my home town of Foxholm, so we had a connection. It was Marie's first time to move with our group, and she was very homesick. She tended to get her work done quickly, which left her with a lot of time on her hands. Often, she'd come and sit for the entire afternoon. I was happy for her when she got to go back home, a little earlier than first planned. Meanwhile, she was kept busy keeping her husband on the straight and narrow. Maynard, a true NoDaker, was a hard worker and a real nice guy who liked his beer. One day after work, he and Don Aarth stopped in for a cold one, which turned into several. While on the way home, Maynard was stopped for running into a pickup that was carrying a load of corn, scattering it all over the intersection. As the cop stepped out of his cruiser, Maynard, more than a little tipsy, called out, "But Officer, the light was green!" Don jerked him by the arm and said, "Shut up you fool. That light was two blocks back!" It took a while for him to live that one down.

Another time, Maynard was picked up for drunk and disorderly conduct and landed up in jail. A short time later, the cops called Marie and told her to come and get her husband. The story was that Maynard had been making too much noise in his cell...running a tin cup up and down the bars! When Marie herded him out the door, there was a cop's motorcycle sitting beside the jail. Maynard drunkenly managed to get on it and insisted that he was going to ride home. I'm not sure he ever lived that one down with Marie.

68

Larry Ferdette was another of our trailer park neighbors. He was a musician, who often played with local bands on weekends. A seemingly single guy, he provided fodder for the trailer park gossip group. Ferdette was also in Rapid City with us. I remember one Boeing management party that we had. After it was over, someone thought it was too early to go home, and we found our way to a redneck dance hall above a bar (we women in our long dresses) where Ferdette and his band, Black Hills Gold, was playing. We ended up closing up the place. we were young.

Al Bushnel was an inspiring singer and a very nice man who was married to a lovely woman. (Millie was one you'd like for a next-door neighbor.) Every time Al had enough money saved up, he would go to Nashville and cut a record. He hadn't made the big time while we were together, but he hadn't given up trying.

Maisie, my bridesmaid, and her husband Ken Meyer and family from Geyser, Montana visited us during the Frontier Days. Living on a ranch, they loved the rodeo with all the cowboys showing their skills. The big parade was also a favorite of theirs. The kids were especially excited when they saw the Budweiser beer wagon, which was pulled by a team of eight huge Clydesdales horses. (They look quite intimidating because of their size, but Clydesdales have a gentle nature.) The horses were perfectly matched with huge fluffy white stockings. To see them come down the street, pulling the shiny beer wagon that was piled high with cases of beer and with a Dalmatian sitting next to the driver, is always impressive. They loved it. During the afternoon, while we were enjoying the festivities, the dreaded tornado sirens suddenly went off. We dashed under the grandstands, where we huddled together until the all-clear signal was given. Three tornadoes had been sighted in our area but, luckily, only one touched down at the North East corner of the city. That slowed down the Frontier Days celebration for a bit, but by that night, everything was back to its rowdy normal.

I was very involved in Jack and Jeff's school while in Cheyenne. I was room mother for Jeff's class, where I also volunteered, and I was secretary of the PTA at their Corlette Elementary School. I was also on the YMCA recreation board. (Jim and I made good use of their facility.) Even though we were temporary citizens, we took part in community affairs.

Boeings' Ed Please, Ray Bitel and Fred Tiegen did their community work when they volunteered to help serving hams in one of the food venues during the Frontier Days. The Chief of Police was also a volunteer. When the Chief pulled out a ham to slice, Tiegen, with his carving knife in hand, rushed forward, "Wait. I'll help you." As he reached to take the ham, he somehow sliced open the Chief of Police's wrist. Blood streamed out. They rushed him to the emergency room where he received five stitches. (To the relief of the volunteers, there were no complaints about bloody ham.)

While in Cheyenne, Mike became an Eagle Scout at age 13, allegedly one of the youngest to ever achieve the rank in the Boy Scout history. That summer, he took it upon himself to prepare his troop for the big upcoming Camporee in Laramie, Wyoming. For two months, he worked daily with the inexperienced group. To the surprise of everyone, including his scout master, the young troop was named the best of all fifty troops that participated, many of which had several Eagle Scouts plus many older boys. We had a reception for him that many of our Boeing "family" attended. During the reception, his scout master presented him a special award for a winning essay he had written about Boy Scout camping food. His prestigious award was a plaque with a cow patty on it.

Mike gained notoriety in another way while there. He and his friend Craig Mattern took out their BB guns, and went hunting for rabbits. They had only been gone a few minutes when I got a call from the military police at the air base. "Do you have a son named Michael?" As they had set out on their hunting trip, the boys crossed a frozen ditch, stepped over a barely visible fence that ran through it and, unknowingly, were then on the air base. They were apprehended on the spot, taken to the military police headquarters, and charged with entering a secure military installation with armed weapons. The base had been on a practice alert when they came upon the intruders, two 13 yr. old boys with BB guns. These boys, who were obviously kids, were treated exactly as if they were international spies! They were interrogated and brow beaten and their guns were confiscated, never to be returned. Ray bailed them out, but not without telling the MPs what he thought about their judgment.

We often played bridge with Ray and Sue Bitel. During one of our games, Sue and I racked up an unbelievable score in just one hand. So high that we posted that score sheet on their fridge where it stayed for the remainder of our stay in Cheyenne! They had doubled our bid, and we confidently redoubled. You bridge players out there know that you have your ducks in order to bid like that, and obviously we did, as we made our bid! We aren't above reminding them of that, yet today, when we're in the middle of a hot game.

Ray, Sue's Ray, obviously played fast pitch softball better than he plays bridge because he pitched a no-hitter on a Boeing team, and also a one-hit game! He was the team's ace in-the-hole.

Ray was also an avid golfer. When he was in Great Falls, he and John Sullivan went golfing at the Malmstrom Air Force Base. When they were on the third hole, John hit his ball into some very closely-spaced trees which, in Ray's opinion,

70

would make for a difficult shot. Ray would have used a seven iron to chip the ball back onto the fairway, but John took a three-wood intending to blast the ball through the trees. He took a mighty swing and all Ray heard was "Bang! Bang!" as the ball hit the trees. It ricocheted back so fast that Ray hardly saw it and slammed into the middle of John's forehead. He went down like a ton of bricks. His eyes rolled back and he appeared to be out cold. Blood ran from his forehead which was emblazoned with an imprint of the Titlist brand. Ray wrapped a towel around John's head, and thinking he might have a concussion and would certainly need stitches, loaded him into his car and headed for the hospital. The doctor took one look at John and said, "Who the hell did this to you?" John was reluctant to say that he had done it to himself but from the look on his face, the doctor had his answer. Knowing that his friend was in good hands, Ray, still chuckling, went back to the golf course and finished his game.

Minuteman Missile personal were very family-orientated and planned fun activities for the kids as well as the adults. Picnics were popular. Shelley Bitel Casagrande's favorite memory was hunting for coins in a haystack. A handful of coins were thrown into the hay and the little kids would be the first to "dig". She remembered how excited she was when she found a whole quarter. "A quarter was a big deal back then," Shelley said.

Shelley's brother Scott was born in Rapid City. Friends, including his Godparents George and Stephany Piontek, gathered for the baptism which took place in the Catholic Cathedral. After the ceremony, Ray was signing the paperwork when he leaned a little too close to the Baptismal candle and set his hair on fire! Caught by surprise, he tried his best to pat it out. No luck! Growing frantic, he thought of dunking his head in the baptismal font but, already embarrassed, he patted it again, this time more aggressively. It worked! The flames were out, leaving him with a burnt forehead and hands, singed eye lashes, and eyebrows that were curled up and frizzled at the ends. The hardest part of all was facing his curious co-workers the next morning. Their laughter was loud and long.

Bitel family: Ray, Sue, Scott, and Shelley

Back to Minot

Cheyenne was finished, and again, out came the boxes. This time we were headed to Minot. We were fortunate to find that the "little green house" was, once again, available. (This house was only a short distance from Minot State University where I had previously earned an associate degree. Mary Lu Wagner and other Boeing people made use of this opportunity and took classes while living there.) My friend Kathy was thrilled to have us back and even living quite close. She and Bob were married before we were, and their children were all older than ours, and then, Jim and Cheryl came along, only months apart. At last, we had kids who could be playmates! Wrong. They wouldn't even look at each other. So much for that idea.

While on site one day, John Musolf called Ray from the base at seven in the morning and told him that the concrete shelter over the site Ray was working on was one and a half feet too far west. The Soviets had spotted it on an over flight and complained to The State Department, who passed the information on to the Air force, and then to Boeing. (The Soviet Union and the US had agreements on what modifications could be made, and they had to adhere to them strictly.) One and a half feet! And it had to be corrected. The result of this was that we now had a greater appreciation of Soviet optics.

Travis Smith was doing construction work in Arkansas when he read an ad in the newspaper. Boeing was hiring for a job on the Minuteman Missile Program. He applied, was hired, and left for Minot the very next day. Travis arrived during a blizzard and subzero temperatures. (When he left Arkansas, it was 90 degrees! He seriously wondered what he had gotten himself into.)

Travis Smith worked three weeks before payday came around. He received no check. New to Boeing, he wasn't sure of the protocol, so he let it go. The second pay period came. Still no check. This time he went into the office and told them that he quit. The surprised personal man asked, "Quit, why would you want to quit?" "Simple," Travis answered, "you don't pay your employees." He promptly received a check for the full amount.

Travis also remembers the time a facility man was told to take care of John Clark's car, which was in sorry need of a good cleaning. Clark was the Operation Manager, the #2 man on the Minot base. The man picked up Clark's blue Ford Galaxy, cleaned and polished until it literally shone. When delivered, Clark opened the door, put one foot in, slid backwards and fell flat on the ground. The entire car, inside and out, had been polished with a silicone spray.

New to this winter stuff, Travis drove an old chevy truck with a heater that didn't work. Big Al Russell car-pooled with him, and it was so cold in the car that they wore their snow mobile suits and had to continually scrape the windows so they could see to drive. That spring, Travis' radiator sprung a leak, and while he was fixing it, he realized the hoses to the heater were on backwards. Once corrected, the heater worked like a charm! They had literally frozen their butts off the entire winter, and all because of reversed heater hoses. To this day, nearly 50 years later, Al won't let Travis forget it.

It was Christmas, and blizzarding, with winds gusting to 60 miles per hour. The temperature was zero. Travis and several of the workers were securing things before leaving for home. They left the base and made it one mile to Ruthville, where one of the transportation drivers lived. Since the roads were closed from there to Minot, they decided that it was a pretty good idea to stay the night where they were.

 At 4 o'clock in the morning, one of the guys got a call from his frantic pregnant wife who was in labor and needed to go to the hospital! The men all checked to see whose car would start in the frigid weather, and the only one that did was Travis's old truck.

The roads were treacherous, and those eleven miles seemed like a hundred. The ditches were filled with dozens of cars that failed to make it and now lay silent as the snow piled up around them. Travis inched by them all. After two hours of grueling travel, the old pickup proudly limped into Minot, one wheel frozen up and the others on the verge. They made it! And just in time-the baby arrived only minutes after the mother was admitted into the hospital.

Again, it was winter in North Dakota, and it didn't let us forget it. This time it was an epic snirt storm, snow mixed with dirt plus wind, lots and lots of wind. Schools rarely have to close in Minot during the winter, as they are prepared for snow, but no one could have prepared for this snirt! Of course, Ray was out on site, and by the time he left, the site trailers were already filling with wet dirt. (It took several days before operations were back to normal.) When he got to the base, his truck wouldn't start. He lifted the hood and found it packed solid with dirt! He'd have to hitch a ride into Minot. By then, visibility was near zero. They drove in a caravan, one car after another, as they inched their way forward. When one car drove into the ditch, six others followed. When he finally got home, he found me making a futile attempt to keep the dirt outside. It had insidiously sifted in

74

around windows and places that we had considered to be air tight. And forget opening a door. I finally gave it up as a lost cause.

That same morning, Holly Triplett's mother, Doris, who was near death in a Minot hospital, called Holly and told her, in no uncertain terms, not to leave the house that day because there was going to be a terrible storm and people were going to die. Thinking her mother might be a little out of it, Holly tried to assure that she would be okay. That wasn't good enough for her dying mother. She wouldn't let it go until Holly promised to stay in. "And if your friend Roger is there, tell him to stay in, too." (Roger Granlund was there along with his roommate Earl Kennedy, plus Holly's two uncles.) Keeping her promise, they settled in for a day of Pinochle. And then it began. A mighty hollowing wind hurled snow mixed with gray dirt, so heavy that you couldn't see across the street. It raged throughout the day and night and temperatures dropped at a rapid pace.

The next morning, the mayor warned people to check their chimneys and asked for volunteers to go out and help those who couldn't. After shoveling the driveway, Roger and the guys worked hours going house to house on several streets and cleaning many chimneys before calling it a day. Later they would say, "If only we had gone one more block." Two elderly people were found dead in their home, just one block from where they had left off. As for Holly's mother, how did she know? Was it a near-death experience? A mother's intuition? A vision? Holly can only wonder.

There were many winter stories, especially when in Minot, but Al and Judy Russell's was a classic! They were living in a Boeing trailer, and one evening Al went to a local bar for a little guy time. A few beers later, he received a frantic call from Judy. "You've got to come home right now, right now! Someone is shooting at us." Al tried to calm her down, so he could understand what she was saying, but all he could make out was, "Someone is shooting at us"! Al rushed out to the car and luckily it started. When he got home, he found a terrified Judy and Little Al huddled down behind the couch. The curtains were crumbled beneath the window, and the long metal curtain rod was lying among ice chunks that littered the floor. (It was the rod hitting the floor that had convinced Judy that they were under attack.) As Al was taking this all in, he heard a loud "Ping!" The water pipes along the floor had busted earlier and ice shards were still shooting up to the ceiling. (Maybe this had something to do with them retiring in Kansas.)

While the ice chunks were flying around in the Russells' trailer, Rex and Linda Howe were packing to leave Minot for their next wing. The morning they left, it was so bitterly cold that ice crystals could be seen floating in the air and the snow crunched beneath their feet.

On their way out of town, they stopped at a restaurant for breakfast. As they went to leave the car, they realized they had a problem-Sambo, the kids' pet turtle. Would he freeze in the car when they went in to eat? Should they smuggle him in? Finally, the decision was made. Sambo, who was in his pan of water, would stay in the car with the motor running. Returning to the car, Travis and Misty quickly checked on their pet and found him surrounded by ice. Fearing the worst with tears already flowing, they frantically dug him out. As he was lifted, his head slowly emerged from his shell. Sambo, the turtle, had escaped the deadly grip of one of North Dakota's worst winters.

Robby Robinson and Jules Rubble were working out of Minot at the Kenmare dispatch area. Jules, a pilot, had his own plane, which he flew back and forth to work. On this certain weekend, he flying to Rapid City to meet relatives who were coming in. Robby was going along for the ride. It was a heavily overcast winter day, and Jules was asked if he had his instrument rating. He assured them that he had penciled it in. A few miles out of Kenmare, the plane went vertically down at regular speed. Both were killed on impact.

Bud Davis, another pilot who worked at the Kenmare dispatch area, flew back and forth from Minot. This one morning when he went to pick up his plane, he discovered that the battery was dead. He spun the prop and it started, but he had forgotten to set the brake. The plane was moving forward right toward a large commercial airline plane that was setting on the tarmac. Davis grabbed a hold of the end of the wing to turn it, and the plane, very appropriately, ended up right in front of the sign that said, "Welcome to Minot."

Some good times were had by some fun-loving guys when they worked in Minot. One incident deserved a Gold Star Award. Five Construction Management guys (Ed Doyle, Jerry George, Terry Helm, "Goose" Gossen and Mike Lewis) stopped at the Ramada Inn one night after work for a quick one before going home to their families. That quick one turned into several happy ones. The Ramada Inn was just across the highway from the Minot Airport, and as they left the bar, they noticed the airport's twinkling sign saying, "Special flights to Vegas" and it just so happened that a Frontier Jet was loading on the tarmac.

Mike said, *"We should go."*

"I think we should," agreed Jerry.

"I don't have enough cash on me," admitted Terry.

"I have my credit card," offered Ed.

"Let's go!" said Goose.

And off they went to Vegas, without giving one thought to calling their wives. The next morning, all sobered-up, reality set in. They called their boss and told him that they would be in for work later that day, or the next, for sure. When they finally got back, they found their desks cleared out and the contents sitting in boxes on top with a big sign on each that said, "Surplus".

It was on to Langdon, North Dakota for Ray. This time the boxes didn't come out as the boys and I stayed in Minot while Ray commuted, a three-hour drive, on weekends. (Many workers commuted from Grand Forks, but some did move to Langdon.)

Langdon, established in the early 1800s by the railroad, was a small town of about 2000 located just 17 miles from the Canadian border. Entering Langdon, one was greeted by the sign, "Standing Proud on The Prairie". When the Boeing people arrived, this sign was nearly covered with snow, and it didn't get any better. Being in an isolated area was a challenge, especially during the winter, when plugging in the tank heaters on the vehicles was as common as plugging in the coffee pot. (It was especially challenging to those who were used to city life in the "tropics".) The Roxy Theater on Main Street, the bowling alley, and several bars-the mainstays of all small towns in North Dakota-were about it, as far as entertainment went...that is, if you could get through the snow to reach them.

Ray found an apartment with John Musolf and Dale Thompson in left-over-housing from an anti-ballistic missile project (ABM) that had once been in operation there.

Ray was on second shift, and one night at about two in the morning, when he and QA Dick Conant were returning to the DA, they witnessed the most impressive natural phenomenon he has ever seen, an aurora borealis, commonly known as Northern Lights. Being from North Dakota, we all have seen Northern Lights, but he said he had never seen any so breath-taking beautiful as the ones he saw that night. Gently changing shafts of shimmering lights danced across the entire sky, lighting it with vibrant shades of pink, yellow, bluish green and purple. As they looked up, they found themselves totally surrounded by extraordinary beauty. Ray was so captivated by it that he called me in the middle of the night to see if they were also above Minot. I crawled out of my warm bed, went out and looked up, but there was only a faint image visible. I had missed nature's spectacular show. Fifty years later, Ray still remembers it in vivid details. Such magnificence is never forgotten.

John Shark and Gary Sinclair were two who commuted from Grand Forks to Langdon. Every day they made the long trip to the DA (dispatch area) where they picked up a government vehicle and drove to the missile site. The ride was long and boring. To entertain themselves, they made wrist rockets and shot ball bearings at road signs to prove their skills. One day they were so intent on their "game" that they got too close to the edge of the soggy road and slide into a steep ditch full of water. They couldn't drive out and the doors were wedged shut so there they sat, out in the middle of nowhere. They had no cell phones but they did have a radio and John put out a call for help, "SHARK IN THE WATER! SHARK IN THE WATER!" After a little maneuvering, they crawled out of the driver's side window and, with sheepish grins on their faces, settled down on the roadside to wait for their rescue.

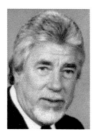

John Shark

Dave McCarville, Frank DeMello, Duane Hauge also commuted from Grand Forks to Langdon and sometimes car-pooled with John. It was the same story-a long boring ride. To make it a little less so, they picked up a few 6-packs for the trip home. Again, they tested their skills. When they emptied a can, they threw it out the window to see who could hit the yellow line and leave it standing upright! Competitors that they were, they kept daily bragging-rights records. They were easily entertained.

John seemed to be the one who kept others entertained. He had spent years on the Apollo Program in Florida and got attuned to the warm sunny weather. When he was transferred to Missouri all that changed, including his suntan. John's wife, Loretta, stayed behind with the kids so they could finish the school term, and John found an apartment above a funeral home that he shared with Stan Pietrzak who was alone for the same reason. Stan remembers the time that John went missing. He wasn't in the apartment, his car was in its usual parking spot, he hadn't left a message, nor had anyone seen him in quite some time. Just when Stan was really becoming concerned, in walked his missing roommate. He's been up on the roof of the funeral home "catching a few rays".

78

John and Loretta Shark

There was a rather scary incident that occurred while they were working out of Minot. An Air Force Missile Crew, while carrying a missile in a transporter erector from the base, took a wrong turn, and accidently ended up in Canada. It wasn't easy trying to turn around towing a missile, and it caused quite a commotion. As nice as Canadians are, bringing the deadliest weapon in the world into a foreign country, uninvited and announced, can have severe consequences. As expected, such events involve the State Department and heads of state. Fortunately, the error was straightened out, and the missile was back on course.

Great Falls, Montana

Great Falls was Ray's next assignment. Once again, the boxes stayed in the basement. Ray left in January, and since Mike and Jack were in high school, it was harder for them to move. Therefore, I stayed In Minot with two teenagers and two younger sons without their father. We made it through until June, and then I cried, "Help!" Out came the boxes, and we packed up once again.

A Boeing trailer was waiting for us, another Magnolia. (It felt like we had come back home.) And once again, Boeing friends were waiting with muscles and dinner. (Someone jokingly said that if a case of beer was mentioned, ten guys suddenly showed up.) Ann and Dave Trepus lived next door to us. Jeff was ecstatic as Steve was his good pal. Ann was a crazy nut who kept things exciting. One Saturday afternoon, she and a gal friend decided to go downtown and ended stopping at a bar for a little Happy Hour, which turned out to be very happy, and Ann felt no pain when she got home. I happened to see the girls outside and asked what their mother was doing. "Oh," they said, "Mom's sick in bed with a terrible flu."

Ann had her own claim to fame. When her husband Dave worked out of Sturgis, South Dakota, she and another Boeing wife, Darlene Neuhauser, organized the first parade of the infamous Sturgis Motorcycle Rally. It was 1973, the earlier years of the rally, and the two women thought there should be a parade. Ann's car had a speaker in it so she, with baby Maureen, and Darlene drove up and down past each motorcycle camp, and loudly announced that there was going to be a parade at such and such a time and where to line up. Everyone loves a parade, and the bikers were happy to oblige. A Boeing man Jim Thanos, who was waiting at the meeting place, took over from there. He organized the line-up and then personally led that first parade. This year, 47 years later, there were 500,000 bikers (down, due of the Covid virus) at the Sturgis Rally. Unfortunately, after many parades that roared down through the hills and on through Rapid City, the parade was eliminated.

Frank and Eva Arias and their family of eight moved along with us. Frank was a QC (Quality Control), and his daughter Lisa remembers that the kids, under no circumstances, were ever to touch his badge and stamp! Being little, she didn't understand the significance of it, but when Dad spoke in that tone of voice, they listened.

They also listened when he whistled. When they were out playing in the trailer park, unsupervised, as all the kids did in those days, they stayed out until either the lights came on, or when they heard their dad's whistle. Frank had a very distinctive one that everyone recognized and if they didn't hear it, their little friends would run and tell them, "Your dad is calling."

The Arias family attended St. Luke Catholic church, as did we, when living in Great Falls. It was much more progressive than any we'd ever attended. Sometimes the singing was a companied by forty to fifty guitars, (Frank played at some masses.) and on certain occasions such as Easter Sunday when my visiting mother attended with us, they went all out. During the offertory women in lovely flowing gowns danced down the aisle playing tambourines to music that soared throughout the church. It was all very beautiful, albeit new to us, and especially to my old German mother, who had attended Mass in little Foxholm, North Dakota with the same German priest for 29 straight years. You can imagine her reaction. Surely, she thought, we had taken her to the wrong church. We still laugh when we think of it.

The Arias children attended a free summer camp that was run by high school kids. When camp was over, the kids, some of them demonstrating their new learned skills, dressed up in costumes and marched in a parade that meandered through downtown Great falls. Vivian, proudly twirling her baton, was dressed as Little Black Sambo, and she won 1st. place! (Today, that would be a big no-no. When I was in first grade, Little Black Sambo was my very favorite book.) Besides bragging rights, the whole family was treated to a free breakfast at the Sambo's Restaurant.

The following memory was sent to me by Frank Arias' daughter, Lisa Britt:

We (Frank and Eva Arias and 8 kids!) moved from Cheyenne, Wyoming to Grand Forks, North Dakota the Thanksgiving of 1975. We ate our Thanksgiving dinner at the Holiday Inn somewhere along the road. Our Dad was driving a U-Haul and there were 4 or 5 little guys with him in the U-Haul, no seat belts back in those days. He was pulling the green Chevy Van behind the U-Haul and our Mom was driving the Mercury with the other kids. The U-Haul ran out of gas just outside of Grand Forks and it was so cold! All 10 of us had to fit in the 2-door Mercury to get to town to get gas for the U-Haul. That is how we made our grand entrance into Grand Forks! We must have looked like a clown car with all those people in it. What I remember is being squished in the back seat, but I was warm! We had to leave Rusty, our dog, in the U-Haul and we cried thinking she would freeze to death. I remember all Mom's house plants were in the back of the U-Haul and they all froze and died. Thankfully, Rusty fared much better, we snuck her into our motel room that night.

Front Row: Vivian, Julie, John, Eva, Frank; Jennifer Back: Lisa, Paul, Carla, Cathy

Lisa told me that having her good friend Lisa Milner with her is what made her moves, and dealing with all the different schools, a positive experience. I believe this to be true for all our kids...their friends moved with them.

Gordy Goodmanson, was working as a supervisor on the flight line in Seattle. The plane he was working on was nearly finished, he was advised to go to Pier 91 to see what job openings were available. He was offered a job in Great Falls, Montana on the Minuteman Missile Program. There was only one catch, he would have to leave immediately. Gordy had never heard of the Minuteman Missile Program, but, he accepted, bought an air-line ticket, and left the next day.

Since he had had such short notice, he was unable to take his family with him. The Bachelor B quarters was not yet available, so he found lodging in the O'Hara Motor Inn, which touted The Sip & Dip Lounge. The lounge had a unique feature, a glass wall between the bar and the swimming pool. Their advertisement said, "Watch swimmers underwater while you sip your beverage. You never know who might turn up, maybe even a mermaid." It made for good conversation.

The Monday after he arrived, he was sent out to the Launch Control Facility. (There was one Launch Control Site Facility for every ten missile sites.) The LCF has a secure underground area that houses the controls to launch the missiles, which are located in the Launch Facilities, or the missile sites as we know them. The controls are located 50 feet underground with a support building topside that housed an eating facility, as well as sleeping quarters, plus other security and maintenance personal. Once the site was activated, there are always two Air Force Officers in the capsule, the required number to activate the missiles.

An hour after he got on site, two Boeing Wheels, Sessions and Popejoy, came to inspect the facility and expected to be shown around. Bob Whitney, his lead man, had been called away leaving Gordy on his own. This was the first time Gordy had ever been on any missile site, and he didn't have a clue, so he just followed them around as they inspected. When they came to the elevator, the door opened, and they all got in. Gordy still didn't say anything. When the elevator stopped, 50 feet down, they got out and turned right which led into the capsule. (A left turn would have led them to the equipment room which maintained the entire area underground.) As they were touring, Sessions *saw* a bar chart on the wall and asked, "Is this bar chart up to date?" Gordy had never ever seen the bar chart, so to be on the safe side, he said, "No." They told him to get it current and left the facility. Two weeks later they came back. The bar chart was nowhere to be seen and was never mentioned.

(When Gordie was working out of Minot, he used to stop in my mother's café in Foxholm for a roast beef dinner!)

Toni and Dick Milner were in Great Falls, too, and one afternoon Toni, another gal and I decided to go golfing at the Country Club. I had never golfed and always wanted to learn so, of course, I agreed. We checked in and went out to the first tee. Toni teed off first, then I took my first swing. At that moment, the golf course manager came rushing out and told us that we had to leave immediately. Seems there was a strike of some kind going on, and no one was allowed on the course. Obviously, the guy in the shop was asleep at the wheel as he had let us in. And I had just made a 200 yd. drive, my first and only. So much for my golfing career.

We did a lot of dancing (and a little partying) in Great Falls, and one of our favorite places to go was knick-named "Menopause Palace." Age-wise, we didn't quite fit in, but they had good dance music, plus good food, which drew us in.

Greg and Renee Ulberg were with us in Great Falls. Renee is my niece and Greg my Whist partner, so I extra happy when he hired on in Minot. Great Falls had some fun places, and I think we found them all. One favorite was the Black Eagle Country Club. It was in a large Italian neighborhood that was full of second-generation immigrants, one of them being Renee and Greg's landlord and wife, Ethel and Rudy Tramelli, who had once lived in the house rented by Greg and Renee. They were a warm and friendly bunch and Renee and Greg soon became "one of the family". When Rudy baked bread, he used to let himself into the house to bake it in their oven, the one he was used to. They always knew he'd been there as there would be a loaf of fresh bread on the table. On Halloween, Renee and Greg took their son Brian Trick or Treating and stopped at the Tramelli's. Ethel said, "You guys don't have to do any more trick or treating" and dumped her entire bowl of treats into Brian's bag. They sat and drank wine for the rest of the evening.

Greg, Renee, Brian, & Tim

Great Falls likes to claim Charlie Pride, one of the few African Americans who became a member of the Grand Ole Opry. Charlie was also a Minor League baseball player, and he moved to Montana in 1960 to play for the Missoula Timberbacks. During his ball-playing years, he pursued his passion for singing by performing in honky-tonks, churches and nightclubs in and around Great Falls. (Gordie Goodmanson remembers buying two C.D.s from him in Great Falls in 1962.)

There were three very good restaurants in that Black Eagle Country Club area-one Chinese, one Italian and The Steak House. The night before Easter, Greg and Renee, Ray and Sue Bitel and Ray and I choose The Steak House, which also had a nice dance floor. It was a night of good food, music and merriment, which ended up at two in the morning with we three women dancing together! (We wore out the guys.) And then Renee had to go home and still fill Easter baskets.

One Saturday afternoon, Ray, Greg and our son Jack were driving down a street in Great Falls when, suddenly, they heard a loud boom followed by a massive fire ball, which hurled upward in a mushroom cloud of smoke and debris...and only a few blocks ahead of them. Startled, they watched as the building seemed to unfold and slowly crumble to the ground. A Charles Bronson movie was being filmed in Los Angeles and they were in need of a building to blow up. Great Falls had just the thing for them, an old school that they were planning to tear down, and the guys just happened to get in on all the action.

Greg has one memory of Great Falls that will stay with him forever. He worked on the Malstrom Air Force Base back in a very secure area known as the vault. It contained top secret material, and a code had to be entered before anyone could enter the area. One afternoon just as Greg was going on break, he pushed open the door and was met with 50 or more people spread-eagle up against the wall, who were being closely guarded by Security Guards with drawn guns. Ed Cynkar had been leaning up against the door, and as Greg pushed it, Ed, a very big man, stumbled a bit and, the next minute Greg found himself with a pistol pointed to his head held by an MP, a very young MP, which made it even scarier. Someone had put in the wrong code, and the silent alarm had been activated, alerting all security and none of the workers.

Another example of the tight security that existed on every base was the time Vice President Spiro Agnew landed at the Rapid City Air Base. Curious, the ETM people stepped out to watch. One of Boeing's subcontractor techs made a wrong move, and immediately found himself surrounded by Secret Service men who were very serious about doing their job. It was a reminder of where they were, and what they were doing.

Lewistown, Montana

From Great Falls, we were transferred to Lewistown, Montana, which was surrounded by the Big Snowy Mountains. Spring Creek ran through it, which added to its natural beauty. The area was known for its great hunting and fishing, which made this move a good one for our boys. Jim, a fourth-grader, liked it so much that he skipped school, forging his parents' names, to go fishing in Spring Creek. When he was walking home, fishing pole in hand, a high school kid speeding down a gravel road, spun out, and kicked up a rock that hit him in the eye. The jig was up. The errant fisherman was taken to an eye doctor and had to have drops put in, several a day, for quite some time. There was no more fishing for our son, during or after school, for, what seemed like forever, to him.

We Boeing wives played softball in a league while in Lewistown-Shirley Mc Carville, Judy Russell, Donna Musolf, Toni Milnor, Julie Johnson and I, to name those I remember. I pitched, and Shirley played second. I can still see her as she scooped up the ball on the run and made the out! (I'm sad to say that both Shirley and Dave have passed away, as have Donna and John Musolf.)

Dave & Shirley McCarville

Donna and John Musolf

I remember our team traveling to another city to play in a tournament. Don, Julie's husband, offered to take one car. During the journey, several of us were in need of a pit stop. Well, there were no rest-stops, so we did what we used to do when I was growing up in rural North Dakota...we got out and used the great outdoors. Later, Don liked to tell that when he stopped and let us out, all he could see beside the car was a row of picturesque white buns.

During one of the games, an all-star player from Helena who wasn't hitting, loudly disagreed several times with the ump's calls saying that my pitches were illegal. The last time she complained, she was ejected from the game. I'm still smirking.

The Boeing Wives softball team

I learned one lesson while pitching-do not wear rings on your gloveless hand. In one hot game, I inadvertently caught a line drive with the wrong hand and ended up with five stitches. I missed several games.

As I was healing, I kept my pitching arm oiled up by shooting pool at the Elks Club. Dick Milnor was my partner and we were pretty good. Ray and Toni were our opponents and they had to stay on their toes to beat us which, I'll admit, they did on occasion. (We had to keep them happy so they'd play with us.)

Red-headed Julie, Don's wife, had a rare eye surgery when we all lived in Small-Town Lewistown-a cornea transplant by a local doctor. (He was local but was a renowned eye surgeon.) The Johnsons were transferred to Sedalia before she was due for a check-up. To solve that problem, the doctor, who flew his own Beech Bonanza, stopped off in Sedalia on his way to one of his practices in another state. Julie met him at the airport, he checked her eye and declared that all was well. She went back home and he resumed his flight.

Lewistown was known for its relatively dry, humid continental climate with long, dry and usually cold winters. When we were there, that cold winter included snow, a lot of snow! Toni remembers hauling kids to two different schools every day. The snow had piled up slowly, day by day, until it covered the first two steps of their porch. (Toni watched this process as it was the way she gaged the amount of snow they had.) When the city snow plows finally cleared the streets, they blocked every side street, making it impossible to get out of the trailer court without shoveling. When Toni finally did get out, she had to battle the snow on the side streets that led to the schools. And then, lo and behold, a nice, long, clear road stretched out before her. Toni barreled ahead! A hundred yards into it, she discovered that the nice, long, clear road was actually a railroad track! A good Samaritan at a nearby gas station saw her predicament and called a wrecker, who rescued her shortly before the next train went through. That was a favorite topic at our great Boeing Reunion in Laughlan, Nevada in 1999.

One weekend while working in Lewistown, Louie Belisle headed toward Jordan on his way home to Grand forks. When he got to the top of the Divide, he ran into a full-blown blizzard. The wind blew furiously, whipping the falling snow into banks, which made driving nearly impossible. He thought if he could only get down into the pine trees, they might block the wind. And then a tow truck that was towing a semi came by. Louie reasoned, if the truck got through, the road must be open. Foiled again! Already it was completely blocked, and he was back to square one. Straining to see through the whirling snow, he saw faint car lights that were heading toward the pine trees. Louie followed. As he drove through the snow, it exploded into a fine powder that seeped into every crevice of the car. It didn't take long before the struggling car gave up and died.

The day had long since faded into night. He dug out a flashlight, and with the wind howling around him, Louie cleaned and dried out the distributor cap, and off he went...for at least two miles. Again, the car died, and once again with flashlight in hand, Louie cleaned the distributor cap. He made several more stops before he finally hit those pine trees, which did cut the wind enough for him to drive on through Montana. It took him three full miserable days to get to Grand Forks, when it usually took eight hours.

It was snowing softly when Roger and Holly Granlund left Lewistown for Sedalia. Holly, singing along with her daughter Kara, was following Roger who was driving the U-Haul truck with its cheery slogan, "Adventures in Moving" emblazoned on the back. As the day wore on, the snow gradually increased until it escalated into a full-blown, white-out blizzard. Gripping the steering wheel, Holly strained to follow Roger's tail-lights which were getting dimmer by the minute. And then, there was nothing ahead but white! Holly grew frantic, "Something must have happened." "Is he in the ditch?" "Did he hit someone?" "Is he dead?" The storm finally let up, and Holly, giddy with relief, could once again see the U-Haul. When asked later how the trip went, Holly emphatically answered, "Adventures in Moving, my ass." "More like Terrors in Moving!"

Holly and Roger Granlund

Sedalia, Missouri

We left Lewistown on Thanksgiving Day in 1978. On the way out of town, we stopped at the hotel for dinner. It was memorable as it was the only holiday meal we've ever eaten in a restaurant.

Back on the road, Ray, in the U-Haul truck, was in the lead towing Mike's '56 Chevy Bel Air. Mike, driving the pick-up, followed him, which left me in the car at the tail end of the caravan. Suddenly, Mike noticed sparks spewing beneath the hitch. He quickly flashed his lights, and Ray pulled over. The ball on the trailer hitch had broken. (The safety chains had kept the car on the road.) As they got out to examine the damage, they looked over the side of the road and down into a canyon that was about 500 feet deep. For a brief moment, both stood transfixed.

Luckily, Ray, being an experienced traveler, had a spare trailer hitch-ball in the truck, and he was able to do the repairs. We were on the road again! Another moving crisis diverted.

Dick Milner was one of the last ones to leave Lewistown. It was his job to close the last site which was located on a gravel road out in the boondocks. A big blizzard had blown through, leaving enormously high drifts, blocking all roads. Dick called Jim Spinks, acting base manager, for help. Since it was a county road, Spinks called the County who sent out an Oshkosh Snow blower. The drifts were so high that even the Oshkosh couldn't budge them. After hours of frustration, they stopped at a ranch and negotiated with the owner who allowed them to open a cattle gate and go through his pasture. Finally, they reached the site and completed their job. Now for their trip back to the base! They had to go through Judith Gap, which was nestled between the Snowy Mountains and the Little Belts and, while beautiful, it was notorious for horizontal winds and bad weather in the best of times. They finally made it back to Lewistown, and it had never looked better. Their families were waiting, (the trailers cleaned and inspected and the U-Hauls all ready to go) and they were on their way to the next base- Sedalia, Missouri.

There was no Boeing trailer court in Sedalia, so we rented a house in South West Village. (This house had been hit by a tornado shortly before we got there, which had done a considerable amount of damage, and right after we left, it was hit again!)

We lived within walking distance of the fairgrounds, of which Sedalia was exceedingly proud. It is listed in the National Register of Historical places as being the oldest fairgrounds in the Nation. Jeff worked at the fair running a kiddie ride. It was his first job. His friend Steve Trepus, a cute kid with a head full of blond curls, also worked there. (The other workers called him "Goldie Locks".) Jim and I used to walk to the fair and would stop at the barns to see the animals. When I think of that fair, I think of the boar pig they were proudly showing. He was absolutely enormous, over a thousand pounds and seven and a half feet long when stretched out on his side. He took up the entire length of the pen! I'd seen many pigs during my lifetime, but this one was something else again, and obviously why I remember this vital fact after all these years.

We gals resumed our ball-playing in Sedalia. After every game, we went to a small bar where we had a beer, ate hamburgers, shot shuffle board, and replayed the game which was as much fun as playing it, well almost. We had gotten pretty good by then, (at least, if you heard us tell we had) and we spent a lot of "serious" time discussing how we did it. (The Alibi Club was the usual hang-out for the Boeing guys, but this little neighborhood bar was perfect for our ball team.)

During a tournament in Smithton, I slide into first base and badly sprained my ankle. I was relegated to the bench and missed playing in the championship game, which, to my dismay, ended my Boeing Wives softball days.

The Party's over!

Boeing management had some excellent parties throughout the years, and the one in Sedalia, a Hawaiian Kon Tiki party, was one of the very best. The open-air gazebo, which was smothered with dozens of tropical flowers, was located out on a pier that jutted out over Spring Creek Lake. The evening temperature was warm and balmy with a gentle breeze that carried the scent of the flowers. There were hula dancers, leis, drinks (with umbrellas, of course), music, dancing, and food- lots of food. They floated an entire roasted pig, all gussied up with an apple in its mouth, on a raft across the lake. The setting sun's reflection on the water was its backdrop as it slowly floated toward us. It was an impressive presentation. A noted chef and his servers, all in Hawaiian attire, waited to carve and served the impressive main course. Yes, it was one of their best parties, and one that is remembered...41 years later.

Ray and I at the Tiki party

Me, Shirley McCarville, and Kay (?)

Renee and Greg and their two little boys, Brian and Tim, lived near us in Sedalia. On Wednesday nights, a few weeks before Thanksgiving, we played Pinochle, kept a running tally of the wins, and who ever lost the most games had to cook Thanksgiving Dinner. Greg and I were Renee and Ray's guests.

Doug and Pam Mar lived next door to The Ulbergs, and they became part of their Boeing family. One of their little girls used to put on her ball glove, knock on Greg and Renee's door and ask, "Can Mr. Ulberg come out and play?" Mr. Ulberg went out and played.

Greg and Renee had a house party to celebrate the completion of Greg's handiwork, a new bar in their basement. (He's a finished carpenter as well as a good card player.) They invited Boeing friends and also some of Renee's friends who worked with her at the telephone company. Rose, who was Black, thanked her for asking but said she had to refuse because Black people could not be seen in the south part of town. (This was in 1978.) A Boeing friend, Q A Russ Ross and his wife, also Black, did attend. The guys were gathered around that new bar during the evening, and Russ just happened to be standing behind it. One of the locals gestured to him, and said, "I'll have a whiskey sour."

When Greg and Doug were transferred to Wichita, their families stayed behind in Sedalia. Renee worked and Pam had kids in school. The guys took turns driving, and on this one occasion, Doug was driving his old Ford truck. In the middle of a rain storm in the dark of night, the windshield wipers gave out and visibility was poor, at best. Greg, with his ingenuity, found some doorbell wire in the truck. He threaded one strand through the left wing-window vent and one through the right window vent, and sitting in the passenger's seat, he operated the wiper by pulling alternately on the wires. All went well until the truck started to drift towards the ditch. Mesmerized by the moving wipers, Doug had nodded off. It was a long 250 miles home.

On October 4, 1979, Pope John Paul II made a historical visit to Des Moines, Iowa. The Pope received a letter from Iowa farmer, Joe Hayes, written at his rural home on the kitchen table, inviting him to travel to Iowa when on his U.S. tour to speak on stewardship of the land. The Pope did just that, and I was there to see him.

The Living Farms, a farmers' organization, prepared for his visit. An 80-foot platform was built out in the rolling hills, special access roads were created, and miles of electric cable were laid. Hundreds of yellow and orange flowers decorated the white oak altar on which the Pope celebrated the outdoor Mass for people of all faiths.

Early in the morning of the fourth, Ann Trepus and I boarded our church bus for our journey to Des Moines. It was a cloudy, rainy, miserable day and we dressed extra warmly as we knew we would be sitting outside.

When we arrived, we found "our seats" on a hillside that overlooked the platform and altar. As we sat huddled together, all we could see was a sea of people, everywhere, 350,000 people from all around the country, the largest crowd in Iowa's history. Some were covered with blankets, others were bunched together under umbrellas, and some even held newspapers over their heads. In spite of our extra clothing, the damp cold air seeped into the very marrow of our bones.

96

And then, we heard that awaited sound, the wup-wup-wup of his helicopter, "Angel One". As the helicopter approached, the heavy clouds parted and, to our amazement, a brilliant sun burst through, flooding the sky with light. All discomfort was forgotten.

As Pope John Paul II , in his flowing white papal vestment, descended from the helicopter, he was engulfed in a shimmering radiance that made it seem like Jesus, himself, had come down to earth. I felt myself holding my breath. A reverent hush fell over the massive crowd, and a sense of peace and tranquility washed over us as he knelt down and kissed the ground, blessing the farmers. (Joe Hayes was among those who were there to greet him and he also assisted in the Mass.)

After the Mass, the Pope entered the helicopter, turned, made the sign of the cross, ("Peace be with you") gave a final wave and was gone-swallowed up by luminous clouds. For a minute, everyone sat, perfectly quiet...and then we all got up and went back to our everyday lives, lives that were never quite the same.

While in Sedalia, we took a road trip to St. Louis to see the St. Louis Arch, the tallest man-made monument in the U.S. and commonly known as "The Gateway to the West." It is a permanent public memorial to the men who made possible the western expansion, particularly Thomas Jefferson, who sent out the great explorers, Louis and Clark. It had only been open to the public a few years when we first visited the Arch. For some reason, we didn't take the 630 ft. tram ride to the top, but I remember standing below and marveling at its height and girth.

Another weekend trip we took was to Silver City on the outskirts of Branson, Missouri. (It got its name from a promotional idea of giving visitors silver dollars in change.) The relatively new theme park was situated at the site of one of one of the earliest Ozark attractions, Marvel Cave. When mining in the cave was exhausted, they put in a railroad, and visitors could ride the train from the cave's depth to the surface, over 200 feet. The boys loved it! Another of their favorites was the Fire-in-the Hole Roller Coaster that went through a dark and scary tunnel that was "on fire". It was all they could talk about on the way home. And me? I remember the many local craftsmen who were doing their thing as we watched. Ray kept me on a leash, but I managed to buy a piece of pottery that I still enjoy.

On another one of our adventures, we stumbled across Burgers' Smokehouse one mile from California, Missouri. We followed the sign, which took us to a farm with a gigantic building that resembled a grain elevator. It was after hours, but the nice owner, Mr. Burger, came out of the house, and gave us a tour. This building was solid full of hams, all kinds of ham hanging from every inch. He took us in an elevator, several stories up, and all we could see were hams. Hams were hanging from the peak of this "elevator", up and down, thousands and thousands of humongous hams. We absolutely couldn't believe our eyes! (The only other smoke house I'd ever seen was my dad's when we lived on a farm. Not quite the same.) As we toured, Mr. Burger explained the curing process that was started by his grandfather, and he ended up selling us a big ham. That was nearly 50 years ago, and today there are many buildings and many more hams all smoked right there at Burgers' Smokehouse.

We took many mini vacations such as these, as they were the perks of our moving. We explored five different states, delved into their cultures, enjoyed their attractions, and ate at their tables. Many became life-long friends. Sedalia, Missouri was the last field assignment for the Minuteman Missile program. Just one more move for the Boeing Gypsies. Ray had his choice. He could go to Seattle and work in the Boeing plant or to Wichita, Kansas. It really wasn't a hard choice, as Seattle was just too big for us small-town NoDakers.

Derby, Kansas 1980

In January 1980, we threw away the boxes (they had earned their rest), said "Good bye" to the U-Haul, and enjoyed the luxury of watching the movers do the packing. We moved into Derby, a small town, which is no longer small, just seven miles south of Wichita and the McConnell Air Base.

Ray worked as a Boeing supervisor in Electronics Manufacturing until peace broke out and then in Facilities for ten years. I planted trees in our yard, substituted in the Derby schools and then went back to college. I taught fifth-grade in Seneca Elementary School in Wichita for two years, Social Studies at the Derby Middle School for the next ten years and then we both retired. Derby, a town we had never heard of before our final move, has been home ever since. Sometimes we miss those moving boxes and smile as we remember. Our days as Boeing Gypsies were unique and interesting… and we wouldn't change a thing.

Boeing Friends at Laughlin Reunion, February 1999

Acknowledgements

Endless thanks to the people who tapped their long-term memory banks and graciously gave me their favorites memories of the Boeing Minuteman program. Without them there would be no book. Thanks to my family for their encouragement and support, especially to my husband Ray who patiently responded time and time again when I cried, "Help!" after pushing the wrong key. And a very special thank-you to Sofia, my granddaughter, who designed the book's cover and to Greg Dye, my technical consultant, who rescued me when it came time to send my manuscript to the publisher. I couldn't have done it without him. I also want to thank my son Jim, who pestered me for years to write this book, "Mom, the Minuteman Missile Program is an important part of history and should be preserved in writing." The time was never right and the years slipped away. And then along came Covid-19 and I discovered that it was exactly the right time to honor his wishes.

About the Author

Myrna Messer was born and raised in Foxholm, North Dakota, a small Midwestern town that has slowly dwindled away. After graduating from high school, she attended Minot Business College in Minot, North Dakota, and then Minot State Teachers College earning an associate degree in elementary education. After teaching several years, she married Ray Messer and retired to raise four sons. The family moved around with The Boeing Company for fifteen years while working on the Minuteman Missile Program and then settled in Derby, Kansas. Myrna returned to college and earned a Bachelor's Degree from Wichita State University and taught for several more years. After retiring, she wrote her first book "remembering...A Town That Was". She now enjoys reading, writing, playing bridge.

At age 88, she says she wrote her last book but there's still a creative gleam in her eyes so we'll see.

Made in the USA
Columbia, SC
11 July 2023

20272398R00066